# Make People Do What You Want

## How to Use Psychology to Influence Human Behavior, Persuade, and Motivate

By: Doug Yimmer

ALL RIGHTS RESERVED

No part of this book may be reproduced, stored in a retrieval system, or transmitted in any form or by any means, electronic, mechanical, photocopying, recording, scanning, or otherwise, without the prior written permission of the publisher.

Limit of Liability/Disclaimer of Warranty: the publisher and the author make no representations or warranties with respect to the accuracy or completeness of the contents of this work and specifically disclaim all warranties, including without limitation warranties of fitness for a particular purpose. No warranty may be created or extended by sales or promotional materials. The advice and strategies contained herein may not be suitable for every situation. This work is sold with the understanding that the publisher is not engaged in rendering medical, legal or other professional advice or services. If professional assistance is required, the services of a competent professional person should be sought. Neither the publisher nor the author shall be liable for damages arising herefrom. The fact that an individual, organization or website is referred to in this work as a citation and/or potential source of further information does not mean that the author or the publisher endorses the information the individuals, organization or website may provide or recommendations they/it may make. Further, readers should be aware that websites listed on this work may have changed or disappeared between when this work was written and when it is read.

# Table of Contents

Introduction .................................................................................... 4

Chapter 1 – Names Are Important! ........................................... 6

Chapter 2 – Hearing the Unsaid ............................................... 20

Chapter 3 – The Growth Mindset ............................................ 36

Chapter 4 – Active Listening .................................................... 52

Chapter 5 – Empowerment in Relationships ......................... 71

Chapter 6 – The Crack in the Liberty Bell ............................. 88

Chapter 7 – Hypnosis and Influence ..................................... 107

Chapter 8 – Persuasion and Influence .................................. 128

Chapter 9 – Summing Up ........................................................ 149

# Introduction

So, how good are you?

That's a scary question for a writer to ask, isn't it? Do you remember your parents telling you that you can be **anyone** you want to be? That's not true, you know. You are human, and as a human, you can only be the beautiful and unique YOU of your dreams and wishes. However....and "however" is the important word here – you don't have to be the "you" that you were last year, or the 18-year-old you once were. That person <u>isn't</u> the YOU of the future. Everyone is good at something, and will get better if they so choose. Everyone can learn to do something new, but <u>if and only if</u> they so choose. Your ability to create and your ability to choose will never, ever, be taken away from you.

Learning didn't stop when you listened to those tediously boring speeches on graduation day...the ones you'll most likely never remember. You cannot help learning, whether you want to or not! Your mind is constantly on the "intake" setting.

So, you want to persuade and convince others? I challenge you...I dare you to do it!

This book includes time-honored techniques that will help you bond with your listeners. Some are tricks to increase your memory, and others are gimmicks used by performers everywhere, but your motives are likely pure and sincere. Some are step-wise progressions leading you through a process that will make you successful. The use of keywords will be emphasized, as they are like triggers for action. This book will be chock full of "true-story" examples, serving as proof that these techniques work.

Extensive discussion is devoted to the body language of your listeners as it holds secrets to tell you more about them. The growth mindset, from the theory of Carol Dweck, is discussed along with ways to change one's mindset for the better. Your mindset is related to the creativity of the mind. Listening skills, as mundane as that sounds, call for a great deal of effort. For a seller, acute listening is essential. It makes the difference between success and failure.

Techniques used in hypnosis will also be discussed here. They are much more subtle and hidden than the mesmerists practice, but not devious. They are proven ways to appeal to people's unconscious minds.

The psychological techniques used by advertisers are elucidated in this book. They influence potential customers' behaviors and can be not only financially rewarding, but will increase self-esteem.

# Chapter 1 – Names Are Important!

> *"A person's name is to that person, the sweetest most important sound in any language."*
> Dale Carnegie

**The Sea of Faces**

Have you ever gone to a party, and the host or hostess introduces you to ten or more people at once? What happens? You lock up, right? Then you wonder if you're wearing the right clothes. You're concerned you won't come across well. Since your parents first corrected you, you learned how to focus on the negatives *first* to determine the approved behavior. The problem with that is the fact that you started by thinking of yourself instead of your target population. That blurs cognition. Instead, focus outward. It is the other person who matters. Ron White, who was the memory champion in 2009 and 2010, said "The reason you don't recall names is you weren't listening." Remember, too, you're not trying to initiate a social interaction. You're starting a conversation.

When you're trying to persuade or motivate anyone to do anything, you need to know who they are. By name! There are techniques for remembering more than one name. Remembering names is important to everyone, and is self-rewarding. It will make you proud of yourself and it will give you a good feeling when you see the positive reaction in others.

## Associative

Each person gives you a visual impression. One facial feature will stand out. Attach the name to that trait. For example:

| Bobby, Bobby the Beak | Sue, Sue the Hair |
|---|---|
| Leroy, Leroy the Mustache | Amy, Amy the Chic |
| Tom, Tom the Vest | Martha, Martha the Sad |
| Elbert, Elbert the Hat | Betty, Betty the Buick |
| Mack, Mack the Bald | Christin, Christin the Eyebrow |

Repeat the name twice, as it will help you remember the name more than you'll remember the feature. Bobby is a long, tall fellow whose nose dominates his face. Sue's the gal whose hair looks like it weighs 20 pounds. Leroy has a prominent mustache, one that looks very different. Amy is a delightful gal who likes to look elegant. Tom is wearing a leather vest. Most people who wear vests wear them nearly daily. It's a symptom of the species! Martha elicits sympathy. It's important to remember, so file it away in your memory bank, as it will be useful when you make your pitch

## Visual

Imagine the person's name emblazoned on their foreheads. Lock onto their face for at least two seconds and mentally print their names upon it. When you're sitting, review the imprinted face-name combinations. Select someone and approach, saying his or her name first. Regardless of whether or not he likes his name, it's still the "sweetest sound" he's heard. We are attached to our names.

Repeat the Name

When you shake their hand, repeat their name. That makes a person feel unique. You know when you've reached first base if they happen to give you their nickname.

"Everybody calls me Augie."

You now have an audience. Typical follow-up questions might include: "What does "Augie' stand for?" It might be "Augustine," to which the Augie might tell you how much he dislikes the name "Augustine."

## The Ebbinghaus Curve of Forgetting

Back in the 19th Century, Hermann Ebbinghaus conducted a study that showed people tend to forget non-complex information very quickly. His study was replicated in 2015 and yielded similar results. It is a fact that information like names is stored in your short-term memory. That's the first to go! The psychologist, George Miller, did a related study in which most people only recalled five to nine unrelated items shortly after they heard them. Stress and lack of sleep contribute to forgetting. So does self-consciousness and introversion.

Have you ever walked into a room in your home and forgotten why you went in there? If you've done a poor job of listening or haven't cleared your "mind clutter" out, it happens.

There are techniques you can use to remember people's names. The major ones cited above were associative, the use of imagery, and auditory techniques. Ebbinghaus and successive researchers have made recommendations to enhance memory improvement. He and the other memory experts have indicated that repetition of the learned material very shortly after it enters your mind can increase your memory 'muscle.' Repetition of the names in your mind helps. Even for a long string of names, your memory might be able to reproduce 75% of them or more. Try reviewing the information within 24 hours.

## The Icebreakers: Jumping to the Emotive

There is a myriad of thought-provoking questions people can ask to launch a conversation. Many of them have been suggested on the Internet, but sound strange or stilted, like "What is your favorite breakfast?" or "What challenges are you facing these days?". "If you could be any kind of animal, which one would you be?"

The least threatening way to start a conversation is the journalistic style. "Where do you live?" "Where do you work?" Yes, they're boring and trite. HOWEVER, what you want to do with those questions is to evoke a feeling. One of the pillars of advertising highlights how the product will make the customer *feel*. If you want to influence people, it's important to learn their likes and dislikes.

For example, "Where do you live?" can lead you to "Do you *like* it there, (person's name)?" That may lead to a "Yes" or "No" answer, or they may tell you why they like or dislike their town. Now you have a springboard for follow-up questions. "How come you (like, dislike) it?"

Watch out! The other may flip the question on you and ask where you live. They are now trying to move you onto the center stage. Your objective is to help the person talk about themselves. So, instead of answering with the logical answer, develop some unique additions to your response like "(name of town)... If you blink, you can't see it" or "(name of town)... I doubt Google has noticed it yet!"

Then immediately return to their zone. "Are your neighbors nasty or nice?" "What's the weirdest thing any of your neighbors have done?" "If you could live anywhere you want, where would that be?" That triggers a wider array of follow-up questions surrounding the person's hobbies, pastimes or a vacation they had. The answer can lead to "What was the funniest thing that happened to you on your vacation?"

Most get-togethers include a snack table. In reality, it often becomes a place to "hide." Have you ever noticed that so many people are silent there? Your goal is to engage another in hopes of developing a relationship and motivate them to do what you want. At the snack table, develop some amusing conversation by asking a question that will invoke humor, like, "Have you ever gone to the grocery store and not recognized something on the fresh produce counter?"

**Keywords**

On the Internet, keywords are words that people type into a search engine. However, people also talk in keywords. Once you have a conversation started, you'll notice how often people repeat them.

You have a pitch to make, and the use of the other person's common expressions will motivate them to 1) like you (because you speak 'their language'), 2) see you, not as a domineering person, but as someone just like them, and 3) as a non-threatening, accepting person who is willing to work with them toward a common goal.

These keywords are subtle psychological techniques that will create a sense of comradery. It is also a leveling device, meaning that you're not trying to come across as too overwhelming or narcissistic. The psychologist Abraham Maslow specified the basic needs everyone has. One of the higher human needs is a sense of belonging and the need for the esteem of others.

Some of these keywords are simply common expressions. Others are words people use to define themselves. Encourage your listeners to elaborate on what they expect of your offering. Identify their interests and ***memorize*** those keywords for later use. Look for the nouns in their speech. Watch their expressions as they speak. Very often, expressions like frowns or smiles will tell you about their values. Someone who frowns and complains about how long a task will take to perform has presented you with a keyword you can use in your pitch to motivate others; like the words – "Fast," "Convenient," and "Easy."

**Influencing Human Behavior**

Rob Jolles, a noted speaker in the area of sales, has said, "If people don't trust you, they won't allow you to influence them.

A smart, simple way to establish trust is to talk less and listen more." In the exercises delineated above, it is your goal to do just that. Recalling names puts you into a position of strength, but your initial conversations are to be non-threatening. The other person is rewarded when you've gifted them with their name.

Establishing trust is related to honesty. Shakespeare has said: "This above all: To thine own self be true. And this must follow as the night the day, Thou canst not be then false to any man."

***Example from Sales:*** Let's say you are trying to sell either a product or an idea. Perhaps one for opening a start-up company selling educational hands-on packages for children. First of all, you have already mapped out the general idea in your mind and know what steps need to be taken to launch it, but you cannot do it alone.

Perhaps it's your objective to get the other person to do a lot of the legwork in your new business. After you've learned the person's name and something about them, you have the tools it takes to make a powerful first impression. The next step is to solicit the other person's feelings. Honesty necessitates that you reveal the idea. However, it doesn't mean you need to explain all the nitty-gritty facts about what the whole job will entail.

Is that being devious? No, and yes. No, because it's likely there will be major and minor changes to your plan as you move along. Yes, because you haven't yet revealed your entire plan. Your idea is an embryo. The characteristics of the final "baby" have yet to be seen. Besides, you hardly want to scare them away. Hitting them with all the complexities you've envisioned would not only scare them away but most likely won't come to fruition in its preconceived form. Your sale is in process, but so is your product.

At your initial approach, you might say: "I've been tossing around this idea about selling educational packages to parents for their children. Instead of the usual digital push-button learning or remote learning, it has to do with craft projects with an educational purpose, like using pieces of cut cardboard to build a 3-D house. It would address hand-eye coordination and the ability to follow directions. So, what do you think?" It's a compliment when you ask someone that.

Wait for the listener's reaction. If positive, he/she will make suggestions or ask you more questions. It makes them feel important, because they are. John Dewey, the noted philosopher, said that everyone has the "desire to be important." Abraham Lincoln himself felt that way. He was a lowly, poverty-stricken grocery clerk who bought books for fifty cents, as he wanted to be greater than he felt. He wanted to speak better; he wanted to attract attention. Nothing attracts attention more than a well-meant compliment. Everyone has an ego that needs stroking. It needs to be sincere, though, and make sense. There's a distinct difference between flattery and appreciation. You appreciate the other person's interest in your idea. You appreciate their time. Most of us think about ourselves. As the other person is speaking, notice their good points. Look at them, their expressions, and even their clothing. Ask questions. Show interest in them. That's why dogs wag their tails when you look at them and hold out your hand to pet them. It shows interest and appreciation in "who they are."

Humans are social beings. We are hard-wired to like other people because they will like you back. Communication is a gift given to humans. Even animals have forms of communication and it promotes them to survive and live happier, more fulfilled lives. We cannot live entirely within ourselves, as no learning or growth would take place. Life would become rather redundant and repetitious.

In 1963, Paul Seeger wrote the satirical song "Little Boxes," which describes life from beginning to end as an exercise in futility. Its lyrics read in part:

> "Little boxes on the hillside
> Little boxes made of ticky tacky
> Little boxes on the hillside
> Little boxes all the same...
>
> And the people in the houses
> All went to the university
> Where they were put into boxes
> And they came out just the same."

Sameness is unnatural. Two trees are never the same. It's uncomfortable, boring, and insane.

Humans create civilizations that generate happiness and peace. Of course, this process isn't without its flaws, but that becomes a challenge. It makes for variety in life. It has its negatives, of course, but can be entertaining and educational.

Most of us spend a great deal of time criticizing things like boring movies, inconvenient but necessary activities, annoying people, the weather, politicians, spam and junk mail. There is a backside to criticizing. The other individual may get the impression that you are a critical person. That's a turn-off.

In your quiet moments, develop some positive statements you can make about life. Avoid talking about your likes and dislikes. Remember, you are being "classified." Try something unusual and amusing. When someone asks, "How are you?" respond with something like, "I'm upright and so are you. That's a plus for the day!"

**Building Trust**

You need to build trust. In the above scenario, the person presented his or her idea. To elicit the other person to do what you want them to do, you need to give them a verbal "gift." When you impart your idea, tell them not to divulge it to others. That will make them feel important. It will make them feel special because you've singled them out from the crowd.

You - as the inventor and creator of the idea - may feel inadequate because you don't have a proven track record. Banish your hesitation! In the *Harvard Business Review*, the social psychologist, Heidi Grant, said, "People are much more impressed, whether they realize it or not, by your potential than by your track record."

Christopher Columbus had potential without an impressive track record. He was just a mariner from Genoa, a city filled with other mariners like him. He was also a cartographer, though a less than adequate one because he was mostly self-taught. While others had sailed around the continent of Africa in the late 15<sup>th</sup> century, Columbus had only sailed as far as the Canary Islands, off the northwestern coast of Africa. He had no proven track record. What's more, Columbus had neither the money nor the sailors nor a ship of his own. Yet, the sovereigns gave him the wherewithal to get that, too! So, how is it that he was able to sell his idea to the mighty monarchs of Spain – King Ferdinand and Queen Isabella?

I have just presented above a story. Dale Carnegie has said that the example teaches. So does the story. According to Paul McDonald of the well-respected staffing firm *Robert Half*, people love stories, so "tell them a story. It also makes it easier for them to remember you later on." Make it a compelling story. Even make it up if your life's experiences don't contribute an example for you. If it's a true story, embroider upon it. Fiction is far more interesting than fact. That's why conspiracy theories are so fascinating. The facts belong to your message and your pitch, but that comes later on.

Design your stories in such a way that your listener wants to hear more. That's also an opportunity for you to entice the listener into contributing to the idea. Later on, he/she can do it on the practical level.

**The Appeal of the Potential**

While tradition dictates that people who highlight their accomplishments will get ahead, that isn't always true. By doing so, you may scare away your prospective partner. He may feel threatened by your perceived competence and feel he might not measure up to the expectations.

People are more attracted to the potential for greatness. It is an unconscious preference inherent in most people. Why is that? Simply because it's less certain. When human beings come across uncertainty, it creates interest and entices them to pay more attention. They want to figure it out. That leads to in-depth thinking and thought processing.

What you've done is make another person sit up and take notice.

The name of this chapter – "No, You Don't Need a Gun!" - quite aptly describes the fact that nonlethal power – the power of the mind – is far more effective in achieving the results you want, whether it be in sales or friendship.

**Dumbing Down the Idea**

In the initial example, the idea about attracting a partner for the start-up business of selling hands-on educational packages to children needs to be presented to your prospective partner simply. Stop there!

Opening up a properly structured business is far more complex, as one must consider such tedious tasks as setting up an LLC (Limited Liability Corporation) or a full corporation with a selected group of stockholders. Finding suppliers and buying from them requires a license under which you can purchase your goods at wholesale prices. Then, of course, there's a need for capital – perhaps through a venture capitalist – and, of course, the money-sucking field of marketing and advertising. The wise choice of a marketer is as important as having a good lawyer when you need one.

Dumbing down your idea is an art form. Avoid jargon, and most of all, avoid acronyms like "LLC." That comes much later. Selling an idea and selling yourself is not a skill; it's a process.

The person you want to hire is going to do a lot of that legwork for you, but they don't know it yet.

**You Are Selling Yourself!**

You might be selling a product; you might be selling an idea. You might be trying to find Mr. or Miss Right. If your listener gives you a compliment, accept it. Most people are afraid that they will come across as narcissists. However, the compliment was freely and honestly given. No one gives holiday gifts back to the gift-giver. When a gift is denied, whether verbal or physical, it denies the giver the right to give it. *Not nice!* Be genuine.

While it is a grand idea to turn the conversation around to focus upon the other person, reserve that for your initial contacts. It's important to reveal something about yourself to the prospect. That serves to impart the impression that you're not hiding anything.

Chatting will help you find common ground with your prospect in your life experiences.

You have solicited suggestions from your prospective partner.

It was originally your idea, but you are not the overlord. Your prospect's ideas might be quite enlightening.

You may feel unsure of yourself because you aren't operating within your comfort zone. That's when doubts creep in. Remember, you've carefully planned your strategy, so trust in it. The process may be slower than you'd like it to be, but one cannot make one spectacular leap into success. You and your projects are works in progress.

Assess what you've done so far; record it. Look at the whole picture. Don't you see there's a difference between where you started and where you are now? That insight will boost your confidence.

Confidence is a *must* in selling yourself, whether it be you selling a gadget, selling an idea or finding your soul mate. There's a worn-out adage: "Believe in yourself." Literally, it's meaningless. *Of course* you believe in yourself! You're here, aren't you? You can touch your arms, your legs, and so on. "Believe in yourself" is a hackneyed term that means self-confidence – the belief that you can do many things, but are capable of doing even more. It is your potential. Believe in your potential.

# Chapter 2 – Hearing the Unsaid

**Listening to the Unsaid**

Everyone communicates non-verbally through their body. 45% of communication is body language. Only between 7 to 10% of the message is in spoken words. When you are trying to win friends and influence others, it's extremely helpful to know what they're "saying," and a good bulk of it happens without words. It is an often overlooked form of communication and goes two ways. Don't forget that you, too, will communicate to others through body language. Here are some visual cues others give you:

1. The Handshake
2. Posture
3. Eyes
4. Arms and Hands
5. Fingers

You can make a general assessment about the other person based on these cues. If you mimic another's movements, you can silently "tell" them that you are interested in them.

**Handshakes**

You want to give the impression of being the dominant one in the discussion, so try to make the first move. Handshakes should be firm, but not too tight. Smile while doing so and make eye contact, but don't stare. Do *not* look down after the handshake. That's a subtle sign of submission. Instead, just glance to one side.

Avoid the fishy handshake. Limp grips are a turn-off. They impart a message of insecurity, lack of self-confidence, and a lack of commitment. If you tend to have sweaty hands, wipe them off. The overt way to do that is clandestinely on your clothing. Hold the person's hand just a tad longer than he does yours...just a tad. Don't latch on! It silently expresses special interest in the other person. Initiate conversation toward the end of the handshake.

Marc Afal, a real-estate salesman in California, once said, "Early in my career I would overlook the importance of a firm handshake and felt that my handshake showed a lower level of confidence, allowing the clients' full control and confidence over the conversation. Clients and colleagues will also be more confident in you being the expert if you are confident about yourself – and a weak handshake shows the opposite."

**Posture**

Where does the person place his weight?

Leaning toward you is a sign of genuine interest. You have their ear. This is the prime time to plant your ideas. It can work both ways, as long as you're not "in their face." If you have a sales pitch, this is your opportune moment. Ask a question relating to their needs and interests. Nod your head in agreement as they speak.

Standing up straight, equally balanced on both feet signals alertness and assertiveness. Watch the person's eyes in this context. A wandering eye means they might be lapsing into boredom. Try speaking ever so slightly louder and say something meaty or valuable. If you're effective, they will shift their weight when you introduce a change of topic.

<u>Leaning against a wall</u> or the top of a chair suggests boredom and disinterest.

<u>Slouching</u> reveals a lack of confidence, disinterest or perhaps just fatigue.

<u>Tilting of the head to one side</u> is also a show of interest. Take advantage of it. Besides, it also may mean they are in the process of thinking and may make a suggestion or ask a question. The latter, in particular, is a very good sign. They're engaged.

Tilting of the head can also be interpreted as an attraction, as the neck is exposed. It shows vulnerability and lack of fear. It is a sign of trust because the other person isn't wary of you and isn't harboring a hidden agenda.

<u>While sitting, a person may rest their head in their hands.</u> Beware! They're bored. Change the topic or ask a question to get them into synchronicity with you.

<u>When one foot is pointed away from you,</u> it may mean the person wants to leave and break off the conversation. Not a good sign! Tell a joke or suggest the two of you go over to the snack tray, have a cup of coffee or something to that effect.

If a person is standing or sitting relatively <u>still</u>, they're interested.

<u>Crossing of the legs while standing</u> can mean interest, as the other person is trying to make themselves comfortable for some time.

Rocking from side to side may mean nervousness, stress or impatience. However, it's important to consider the fact that all people have to shift their weight from time to time.

The fig-leaf pose refers to the bodily position when a person holds their hands together in front of their genitals. It can signal the presence of embarrassment or introversion.

**Eyes**

Oculesics is the study of kinesthetics related to eye movements, gaze, and related behavior of the eyes. Behind the eyes lies a wealth of information about an individual. With a little study, you can learn to influence others because their eyes will "tell" you what they're thinking and how they're reacting to your words. Once you can get a handle on that, you can mold your conversation to get the other person to respond positively to you.

Psychologists tell us that maintaining eye contact is good, as it shows interest and sincerity. Of course, that doesn't mean you should lock into a stare. Staring is aggressive or can be silently read as a sign of deception. Be wary if you notice it in your listener. When you look at a person, focus instead on the bridge of the nose, just between their eyes. That will come across perceptually that you're looking at both of the eyes simultaneously. It will help you avoid shifting your focus from one eye to the other, which can be rather distracting to the person you're interacting with.

Avoid maintaining eye contact constantly. Glance away from time to time. When you look at the eyes, you are "peeking" into the mind of the other person. That's a tiny "invasion" into personal place. But *do* use it to drive an important point home.

Chapter 8 goes further in-depth on that issue because there's more to that than one may initially assume.

<u>Blinking</u> is a sign of nervous tension and stress unless caused by a physical condition. Your listener(s) might also be afraid or worried, in which case you don't have their full attention.

<u>The directionality of the gaze</u> may indicate that they want to go to another part of the room or leave. You've lost them. If they're looking toward the snack table, you might still have a chance to engage, but don't count on it!

<u>Looking down</u> may indicate that the other person is working through a problem. They're distracted. However, don't jump to that conclusion too quickly. They might be remembering something related to the topic you're discussing.

Some people tend to <u>look up</u> at the ceiling as they chat. Yes, it's rather disconcerting, but it may simply mean they're mulling a thought over and preparing what they want to say next.

The <u>unfocused eye</u> is a sign of boredom. If you see that in your listener, say something to regain his or her attention. You can also drop your cell phone suddenly or make an unexpected noise.

The <u>glaring eye</u> might mean anger or envy. Carefully guide your conversation to relax the other person and communicate in such a way that they feel you're on their side.

<u>Pupil dilation</u> is an excellent sign of great interest and curiosity. Pupil constriction shows a lack of receptivity.

A furrowed brow means concentration. If you see slight marks of a person having furrowed their brows often, they are thinkers who pay close attention.

Raised eyebrows can be a sign of discomfort.

Looking "past" you toward other people in a group setting means that the person isn't interested in talking to you. Back out gracefully. You can't win them all!

Eye Blocking or putting their hand or hands to their eyes occurs when someone is irritated.

Squinting may mean dislike, non-belief or suspicion. On the other hand, it can be a sign that the person is confused about what was said.

Looking intently means the person is concentrating. Good sign!

**Arms and Hands**

It's quite true that many people gesture - that is, "talk with their arms and hands." This trait is often demonstrated by gregarious, out-going people. Gestures are used for the sake of emphasis, but may also be engaged if a person feels that you may not quite understand what they're saying.

Open, outstretched hands with the palms up are a positive sign. They're interested and interesting. They glory in attention, so give it to them. That will please them greatly, and you're on your way to winning a friend if you remember to follow up with them.

Clenched fists mean hostility or frustration. It is an automatic outcome when the hormone adrenalin races through the body.

Crossing the arms is *not* usually a sign of rejection. That's a myth most people believe. According to Joe Navarro, the ultimate expert in body language, it is a self-soothing behavior and an attempt to feel secure.

Another misconception, Navarro added, is the belief that when someone covers a part of the face briefly, as in touching the eyes, mouth or cheek, it means deception. It does not! This action, too, is self-soothing. He also added that "As human beings, we are lousy at detecting deception!"

Arms akimbo (placing one's hands on the hips) means the person is becoming territorial or is evaluating what was said critically. It may also telegraph arrogance.

If finger-spacing is wide, the person is confident and open. If space closes up, it could mean the person is stressing out. Steepling of the fingers may mean the person feels less confident, and that can be used by you as a cue to discuss the issue more or ask the person for their reaction.

Finger or foot drumming is sometimes a sign of boredom. The other person can't wait till the conversation is over.

Finger-pointing shows dominance or accusation. It is subtle bullying behavior. However, when a finger is pointed at a member of an audience, it's a personal sign of recognition, even if the speaker doesn't know the listener. In that case, it's not hostile. Politicians use this to signal respect for a friend, and give the impression that they know a lot of important people. Keep an eye out for it when you next see a political speech. It works!

<u>Rubbing the hands</u> together can mean the person is about to tackle a thought they have or react to what you just said. If excessive, though, it can indicate stress. Of course, take the weather into account, as it will happen if the person is simply cold! Ask if your listeners are comfortable and, if not, have someone raise the thermostat. That will give them the impression that you "take charge".

<u>Pulling on the ear lobe</u> may mean a person is trying to make a decision. (Or it's simply itchy!)

<u>Hands in the pockets</u> implies that the person is hiding something. Some people seem to feel that it's a sign of being casual, but – if so – it's a fake gesture.

## Mirroring

Oscar Wilde once said, "Imitation is the sincerest form of flattery that mediocrity can pay to greatness."

Human beings use mimicry to respond to events and also to express their emotions. Most people prefer to keep their emotive responses to themselves, but their bodies will betray them. If you learn how to read those subtle signs, you'll be able to recognize how people are responding to you or others. When people want approval, they will attempt to mimic the actions and even the appearance of those they want to impress.

If the boss is acting formally, his staff will conform. If he is more casual, his employees will do the same. It has the effect of creating a bond among the people present. The staff, too, hope they will receive the approval of the boss by mirroring. Now, if someone joins the meeting and puts his feet up on the table, he will draw negative attention, frowns, fiery stares, and even sarcastic remarks.

Speakers can gain trust and support if they mirror the behavior of others. Suppose a speaker arrives at the group he's about to address in a three-piece suit. Suppose all the people in the group are dressed casually and even hang their arms over the back of their chairs. Most alert speakers will notice that. Then they will take off their jacket and loosen their tie. Their audience will non-verbally get the message that the speaker isn't arrogant, nor does he consider himself superior to his audience. He is the speaker who will get more questions at the end, indicating that he aroused curiosity and heightened the audience's interest.

When people feel hostile or disagree with the one who is speaking, their movements will be less coordinated. Their movements won't be smooth. Random movements, when unexpected, also signal signs of a conflict between the speaker and the listener.

Researchers have experimented with the effects of mimicry. In all of the studies, they discovered that the people who were mimicked were far more likely to buy products from those who imitated their behavior and body language than those who didn't. It's a very subtle practice that goes virtually unnoticed, but has proven to be very effective.

In a 2007 study by the social psychologist Dr. Nicholas Gueguen, speed-dating was used to evaluate the effect of mimicry in body language and even verbal expressions. It was found that the men in the study asked to see the women who mimicked their facial expressions and movements during the interview more often than those women who didn't. Therefore, it wasn't the impact of the content of their verbal interaction that attracted the men, it was their non-verbal messaging.

When you want to influence another person or persuade them, carefully watch their body language. Mimic it, but do so subtly. It is a means of gaining rapport and eliciting trust. In a subconscious way, it's a compliment. It communicates to the other person that he or she is on the same "wavelength" as you are. That person is a friend.

If the other responds with a lot of face touching, hand touching, and leaning away, they're not responding well and may mistrust what you're saying, or it's simply an abbreviated form of self-stroking, a security tactic.

Watch for contradictions. Have you ever noticed people who are trying to make a positive point, but they're turning their heads as if to say no? That happens quite frequently. You'll see it on TV shows quite often and it is a dead giveaway that the person is acting. Politicians do it frequently, and it may signal the fact that there are caveats to what they are saying or promising.

Try to be congruent at all times.

Suppose a woman is presenting a proposal to a small group of potential investors. The idea she is going to present is a good solid one, original, creative, and potentially profitable. She's dressed attractively in business attire and has one hand in the pocket of her jacket. Every time she's making a point, she turns slightly sideways. When she wants to emphasize something, she stops abruptly and points her finger straight at her audience. She keeps shifting her weight from one side to the other as she speaks and her eyes dart back and forth like a ping-pong ball when she looks at her audience.

If you were to eliminate the verbal content, what is she *really* saying? Let's break it down:

She's dressed attractively in business attire and has one hand in the pocket of her jacket.

*(What's she trying to hide?)*

Every time she's making a point, she turns slightly sideways.

*(Yo-hoo! We're over here! Make eye contact with us!)*

When she wants to emphasize something, she stops abruptly and points her finger straight at her audience.

*(Yikes! What did we do wrong?)*

She keeps shifting her weight from one side to the other as she speaks and her eyes dart back and forth like a ping-pong ball when she looks at her audience.

## The Problem with Words

As was said earlier, 7 to 10% of sales are words. Words can get people into trouble.

There was once a salesman in the Midwest who tried his hand at selling trucks. He felt that his trucks were superb and were his own products. Sincere belief in your product is a very admirable trait. However, that belief backfired on Carl, the truck salesman. Even though he believed in his product, he managed to antagonize his customers. How did that happen? How *could* it happen?

> True Story: Carl's Trucks
>
> Carl had a job selling trucks. He took the position because he himself owned one of those trucks and was very impressed with its performance and style. Carl really believed in his product. Unfortunately, he felt that everyone *else* should be just as convinced of it as he was.
>
> If a potential customer came into his showroom and said anything derogatory about that particular truck, Carl would become deeply offended! He told the customer how wrong he was and the arguments accelerated. In the end, Carl won the arguments. He felt good because he was right and knew he was right. He even bragged about it to the other salesmen.
>
> Carl's colleagues were horrified. Carl may have felt he won the arguments, but — of course — was unable to change the customers' minds. It didn't matter if Carl was right, he was just as futile as if he were wrong.

If you're wiser than the other person, never tell them so. Let them discover your idea, believing it's their own.

Instead, listen to the customer. Be open and interested in his opinion. Encourage him to elaborate upon his thoughts. Look for areas on which you do agree with the person and elaborate upon them.

If a prospect makes eye contact with you and/or the product or proposal, between 60 to 70% of the time, they're not only interested in what you're selling or saying, but they tend to agree with you. They may need time to ask questions or express concerns, so it is your role to relax and not exert pressure. They need the stage; they need to feel important.

## Example: Selling a Vehicle

We'll use a scenario here in which a person thinks they might want to buy an SUV. The customer walks into the showroom and wanders about looking at the various SUVs he sees. You're watching from a discreet distance. The customer hesitates at a red truck, then places his hands on his hips.
Interpretation: The customer is critiquing the vehicle.

He looks at the truck intently, with pupils dilated, and stares inside the vehicle.
Interpretation: Pupil dilation means interest and curiosity.

You: "That's one of my favorite models on the floor."

You know the customer is curious, so you already know he'll start asking questions.

Customer: "Is it a two-wheel drive or a 4-wheel drive?"

You: "Two-wheel drive. It's very good on gas."

Customer: Looks around the showroom.
Interpretation: He's lost interest in the red truck. You now know that he may want a 4-wheel drive, so you lead him to another truck – a 4-wheel drive lime green one.

Customer squints.

Interpretation: The customer is displeased or has issues. The color may be turning him off.

You: "You don't like the color, do you? That kind of annoyed me, too. What do you think about the GPS feature? It seems to be easy to operate." You hold the door open and point out the GPS screen and demonstrate how it works.
Interpretation: You've shifted his focus away from the undesirable trait and gotten his attention on an easy-to-operate tool.

The customer <u>looks intently</u> at the GPS screen and punches a few buttons.
Interpretation: He's very interested in that feature, so you can capitalize on it.

You: "The screen also shows the proximity of other vehicles. It beeps when you're too close to something behind you. That's very helpful when you're backing up."

The customer puts his two hands on the steering wheel.
Interpretation: He wants to take a trial drive.

You: "Let's take it for a spin. What do you think?"

Customer nods.

You then get the keys, climb in, and he pulls out of the front parking lot. You direct him around the back where he can move in front of another vehicle. Then you instruct him to back up a tad. He does so and the screen shows the vehicle in the back. He backs up slowly. The screen beeps. The customer smiles and stops.

You, knowing that the color isn't pleasing to him, lead him back to the red truck.

You: "What do you plan on carrying in the truck?"

Customer: "Mostly washing machine parts."

You: "Do you think the red truck could handle those?"

Customer: "This 2-wheel drive will save on gas mileage, too."

You: "Good point."

****

The customer has now sold himself the truck, with a little assistance from your ability to read his body language.

# Chapter 3 – The Growth Mindset

Carol Dweck, the clinical psychologist, who was known for her work on the growth mindset and the fixed mindset, presented a theory by which a person could learn how to modify their approach to mold those with whom she came into contact. People with a growth mindset are far more adaptable and can relate to others persuasively. That is not to say that people with a fixed mindset cannot persuade others. It also does *not* mean that those with a fixed mindset can't modify their world view. In addition, certain audiences gravitate more toward the steadiness and predictability of those speakers with a mostly fixed mindset. It gives them a sense of security.

Dweck presented the questionnaire below to determine how you relate to the outside world, and the answers to those questions can predict how successful you can be. The ideal classification is the growth mindset, according to Dweck, but there are exceptions to that. Dweck indicated that with the growth mindset one can accomplish more, can become a persuasive and influential person, and experience a great deal of success in influencing others and creating a following. That, in itself, is a reward.

Exercise A: Take a look at the questions Dweck asks about your beliefs about intelligence and answer them honestly to yourself:

> 1. "Your intelligence is something very basic about you that you can't change very much."
> 2. "You can learn new things, but you can't change how intelligent you are."
> 3. "No matter how much intelligence you have, you can always change it quite a bit."
> 4. "You can always change substantially how intelligent you are."

Exercise B: Take a look at the questions Dweck asks about your abilities and answer them honestly to yourself:

> 1. "You are a certain kind of person and there is not much that can be done to change that."
> 2. "No matter what kind of a person you are, you can always change substantially."
> 3. "You can do things differently, but the important parts of who you are can't be changed."
> 4. "You can always change basic things about the kind of person you are."

In Exercise A, people who chose # 1 and # 2 are of the fixed mindset. Questions # 3 and # 4 are growth mindset people. In Exercise B, # 1 and # 3 are fixed mindset descriptions and # 2 and # 4 are growth mindset descriptions.

How you rate on those personality traits reveals how you relate to the outside world. People who are more apt to improve their skills and become other-directed, carry within them the qualities of a growth mindset. Those who have a fixed mindset tend to focus on what others think about them and/or their product or service.

A person with a fixed mindset perennially tries to prove him or herself. They're oversensitive to making mistakes. That, unfortunately, tends to be a self-fulfilling prophecy, as they do make more mistakes due to their high anxiety. Those with a growth mindset, on the other hand, actually make fewer mistakes, as they don't feel as if they have a giant magnifying glass on them. Their minds are freed up enough to think clearly.

In an experiment, Carol Dweck presented two groups of people – one group were "fixed-mindset" people, and the other group were "growth mindset" people – with the task of running and managing a furniture company. The variable factors of intelligence and ability set were the same for both groups. At the end of the experiment, those with the growth mindset outperformed those of the fixed mindset.

People who are of a fixed mindset often tend to be what is called "yes men." What they do is deprive themselves of the use of their ability to think for themselves, and "pay homage" to the prevailing opinion of the masses.

---

True Story:     When Nate Laughs

In a small parking garage in Boston, Leroy took a job. He and the guys who worked there would come across Nate, the boss, at night when he came in to check on the receipts for the day.

> Nate tended to tell jokes, but the jokes were corny. Not funny at all. Nate, though, enjoyed his jokes immensely and laughed heartily. Whenever Nate told a joke – and he told many – everybody in the garage laughed just as heartily as Nate did.
>
> Leroy was astonished at that, as not a single so-called joke was even slightly amusing. After Leroy went through one of those laughing sessions, he asked his co-worker, Ralph, "When Nate told those jokes, I didn't find them funny at all. Why did you?"
>
> "Leroy," Ralph replied, "When Nate laughs, everybody laughs."
>
> If you didn't laugh at Nate's jokes, he took great offense, as he pictured himself as the comedian of Boston. During the next session, Leroy laughed just like everybody else. He laughed heartily and long. That is how Leroy survived the job.

## You Don't Have to be Fixed!

Regardless of your age or station in life, you can change. Your attitude toward life and your ability to be a moving force in your world of operation aren't "fixed" in stone! You're not condemned by some imaginary crystal ball to fulfill a deadpan fate. The traits you have aren't ones you have to live with for the rest of your life. The "hand you're dealt," so to speak, can be a starting point. The more positive ones can be cultivated like flowers. You don't always have to grow on your own. Others you meet can help.

A person's true potential is unknown. Today's greatest singers and actors weren't born on stage. Many went the long, hard route of countless auditions. They went to New York or Hollywood, rented ratty rooms in shabby hotels to go to the next audition. Dancers spent many painful nights nurturing their sore muscles after hours of grueling exercise. Ballet dancers stretched their bodies into contorted positions until they could hold a pose for minutes on end.

People with the growth mindset are willing to learn. They don't stall out and conclude they're not capable of more. A setback isn't an end.

Have you ever gotten fired? Many of you reading this may have. Take a look at yourself today. Are you working? Of course you are! How many of you now have jobs far better than the one you were fired from? Four processes can occur after you were fired: 1) you realize you made a mistake, 2) you realize it wasn't the end of the world, 3) you learn from the experience, or 4) you *fail to learn* from the experience. People with a fixed mindset become depressed and leave with their tails between their legs. They don't care. Why not?

Humans, by nature, are curious. There's a reason for that. In the 1970s, Arno Penzias and Robert Wilson were working on developing a radio receiver. They set up their equipment in a field in Holmdel, New Jersey. When they listened, they heard a noise they couldn't explain. As they explored their tube-like device, they found pigeon and bat droppings inside. So, they crawled inside the device and removed that. The noise was still there.

Did they give up? Did they assume they failed? No! They were curious. After many successive trials, the noise remained. As they investigated, they carefully eliminated all other possible causes for the noise. After consulting with Robert Dicke, a respected astronomer and physicist, they realized that they had discovered cosmic microwave background radiation emanating from a remnant of the Big Bang – which kicked off the evolution of the universe. For that discovery, they won the Nobel Prize in 1978.

There are many rewards for curiosity. People with fixed mindsets have no interest in learning from their mistakes. They cringe if they're given feedback. They're not curious and they close their minds to challenges. Hence, they shut down and don't learn. They avoid what makes life interesting. How boring! Those with fixed mindsets can and do develop curiosity...especially those with children.

No one will discover their full potential if they're not curious enough to find out what that might be. Be curious!

**The Power of Choice**

If you want to be a persuasive person – a "shaker" and a "mover," you're not born that way. We are all born with basic needs as a child, but you want to become an adult. You can become a carbon copy of your parents, and some children grow up to become their parents. In time, they are horrified when they look in the mirror and realize what's happened. There's nothing wrong with being *like* your parents, but it's not helpful to *become* your parents. Even your parents want to see you become better and different than they are. They know their shortcomings and certainly don't want to see you repeat them. It's an exciting thing for them to discover that you manifest a quality that surprises them, like an engineer and a lawyer who have a child with terrific artistic ability.

Society has the unfortunate tendency to be negative. It is full of warnings like 'don't pass on the right or you'll break a traffic rule,' 'no parking,' 'don't litter.' 'You shouldn't eat too many carbohydrates,' 'you shouldn't eat too much red meat.' The world is full of "Don'ts" and "Shouldn'ts'." We are all conditioned to the negatives in life. No wonder the fixed mindset is so strong. It's safe, but it's monotone. No wonder our limitations shine out in our heads like flashing neon signs. No wonder they have the power to tempt people into concluding they can't change.

Many people are inflicted with the negative in life. As soon as someone proposes that a person with a fixed mindset do something challenging, something different, their first reaction is *"I can't!"* Mind you, they haven't even tried yet. However, it's different and it's the difference that frightens them....yes, *frightens* them. But they can do it if they so choose.

### Neuroplasticity

The brain isn't fixed. It's constantly changing, regardless of age. Professor Cruz Eusebio from the Chicago School of Professional Psychology has said, "People who learn new skills are people who become more intelligent." While it has long been believed that IQ is permanent, recent research has noted that people can yield higher IQ scores if they exercise novel ways of doing things. Here, the professor is referring to what is known as "fluid intelligence." A person with a fixed mindset performs activities in routine ways. Fluid intelligence is the ability to reason through projects or problems in unique ways. Those with a fixed mindset don't make use of their ability to use fluid intelligence. They are routinized.

The brain is made up of neurons that forever fire impulses one to the other. Each is surrounded by a myelin sheath, and when more blood flows into the brain, the more this myelin sheath is nourished, providing more strength to the neurons. People who think a great deal, increase the ability of these nerve cells to "communicate" with each other. That stimulates the growth of more neurons. Neurons can then form new neural networks. Thus a new pathway is formed. In pedestrian terms, that means a unique thought is created. The thought then races to the conscious thinking part of the brain, called the "neo-cortex."

In a controlled study using rodents, some rodents had an interesting environment in their cages — wheels, little huts, twirling objects, and the like. The other rodents had a plain environment without toys or interesting shapes. In an autopsy of their brains, the rodents with the plain environment had little anatomical differentiation. Those rodents who had the enriched environment had a more developed brain, full of convolutions and subdivisions. This was a monumental discovery and proved that the brain can change and grow with challenge and the use of fluid intelligence.

People with a growth mindset have developed new neural pathways, resulting in creative approaches to their work or their projects. It's exciting to work with such people, and it's stimulating to listen to them. They are the ones who create interest and draw a following. Moreover, they are the ones who can influence others.

## Changes in the Brain

The field of neuroscience is a freshly developing area of study. Neuroscientists are fascinated with neuroplasticity. There is some actual measurable proof that people exercise their brains in new and unique ways. You've all heard of MRIs (Magnetic Resonance Imaging). MRIs are used to "map" the brain of people with strokes or cranial cysts. However, MRIs are also used in studies of neuroplasticity.

In numerous studies, special dyes were inserted into the brain. During selected mental exercises, certain areas of the brain "light up," and can be recorded in an MRI. Over time, those MRIs revealed a thickening of cortical (brain) tissue. The brain developed more convolutions and expanded in certain areas. That is what occurred during the test of rodents cited earlier. The brains of the under-stimulated rodents showed little differentiation, but the brains of the stimulated rodents were more developed.

The neuroscientists also discovered that the brain produces a molecule produced nowhere else in the body. It is called the BDNF, or "Brain-Derived Neurotropic Factor." More BDNF molecules produced by the brain increase cognition and long-term memory.

The same thing happens to the person with the growth mindset. The famous novelist, Stephen Cannell once indicated that, at one time, ideas for new books came rushing into his mind faster than he could write them down. Cannell had to develop a system to keep track so he had plenty to write in the future. He then became a TV producer and was a multimillionaire when he died. Nurturing a growth mindset can be quite profitable.

## How to Develop a Growth Mindset

The growth mindset has to do with attitude and self-image. Of course, it's easy to read this, nod your head, and tell yourself you're going to start doing that today. However, a change of attitude isn't easy. It takes practice…practice…practice. Here's how you can start:

1. Embrace Challenges
   If you look upon an attempt to try something new as an opportunity, you can change your attitude towards it.
2. Listen to Yourself
   Each person has a little voice within them. Every day it directs their body and actions. Judge your thoughts as they come tumbling out. Many people enter a social situation pre-convinced that they aren't wearing the right clothes, will say something stupid or shudder in fear that no one will like them. Those are negative thoughts. Negative thoughts have a nasty way of becoming self-fulfilling prophecies.

   Judge each of your thoughts as either negative or positive. Every time a negative thought slips out, immediately substitute it with a positive thought. That's not easy to do, is it?
3. You Are Who You Are
   No one can claim to be the greatest wonder the world has ever seen, so they would be far better off if they accept themselves for who they are. That's not a

verdict, by the way. One can change in time and become better than they were *yesterday*. So, you are who you are today, and can be better than you were. That is the blessing of time and growth.

That is called self-acceptance. You are not perfect, but that doesn't make you a bad person. Remember that always.

There's an old cartoon that first aired in 1919 about the character Popeye the Sailorman. He was not a good-looking guy but he knew who he was and knew what he could be:

> "I yam what I yam
> 'cause that's what I yam…
> I'm Popeye the Sailorman!"

4. Take Off the Mask

   Stop making believe you're someone else. What happens if you pretend, is that you have lost respect for yourself. You don't deserve that. Besides, others will immediately know you're masquerading. It is far better to be authentic, but never, never put yourself down. Statements like, "Oh, I can't do that," or "I really, really stink at \_\_\_\_\_" should be wiped from your vocabulary.

5. What Is Your Purpose?

   What drives you? Don't say "work." That's too general. What about work? How is it going to be different today? What do you want out of a life where you find yourself today? Set a goal – short-term or otherwise.

6. It's the Process that Counts

    You may have set a goal for the day or the week, but didn't accomplish it. More important than the goal is the *process*. The thoughts you had were well worth thinking. They exercised your brain. It kept you moving through the day. You can pick up where you left off and continue.

    When you travel somewhere, you tend to look around, derive conclusions about what you see, and note curious objects you may have not seen the last time you journeyed. When you get home, you will recall more than just the destination; you will remember the many things you observed while you traveled. The process, the journey, is just as important as the destination.

7. Exercise

    For a lot of people, that's a naughty word. However, the brain needs blood flow. New neurons develop if they're lubricated by blood. The National Institute of Health indicates that aerobic exercise promotes the growth of new brain cells. Tests have been conducted both after a period of exercise and non-exercise. In studies, MRIs were compared between people who had just finished an exercise session and those who didn't. Results showed that the people who had just exercised showed a difference in the areas of the brain related to cognition and memory.

The exercise need not be strenuous. Simply walking increases blood flow to the brain and the cognition centers of the mind. In 1889, the philosopher, Friederich Nietzsche wrote, "All truly great thoughts are conceived by walking." Studies have shown that walking causes an increase in the neurotrophic factor, BDNF, the molecule that accelerates the thought process.

8. Coupled with Challenges Comes the Fear of Failure
If you again reframe your thinking, you can look upon the opportunity or challenge as a means to learn something new. When one learns something new, they don't expect to do it perfectly. You will automatically make allowances for yourself. The activity in question then becomes a learning experience, not an abysmal failure.

---

True Story: An Ice Skating Experience

Nine-year-old Caitlin wanted to learn how to ice skate, so her sister, Natalie, dressed her in a heavy Parka and took her to the rink. Initially, Caitlin refused to enter the rink. Instead, she looked at all the other people skating. Carefully, she studied all their moves and watched their rhythm as they moved around the rink. Then she entered. Natalie offered to help, but Caitlin wouldn't let her do that. Then Caitlin kicked off the side and went around and around without falling. Natalie was astonished. After doing that for nearly half an hour, Caitlin pulled off to the side.

"That was terrific, Caitlin," said Natalie.

> Next, Caitlin kicked off and started skating again. Then she fell. She picked herself up afterward, skated a few feet, and then fell again. She repeated that but kept falling. After about twenty minutes she pulled up at the edge of the rink.
>
> "What happened?" asked Natalie who had seen Caitlin perform perfectly in the earlier session.
>
> "I became so afraid of falling, that I decided to fall to go through the experience. Now I'm not afraid of falling."

What Caitlin did was to reduce her fear of failure by permitting herself to fail. Afterward, she realized that failure wasn't as disastrous as she imagined it. There was wisdom in doing that. Permit yourself to fail.

## The Growth Mindset, Creativity, and Change

The term "creativity" isn't simply reserved for artists, poets or writers. Creativity is a mental process that leads to concepts, solutions, and products or projects that are unique and novel. Albert Einstein himself once said, "Imagination is more important than knowledge. For, while knowledge defines all we currently know and understand, imagination points to all we might discover and create."

Mathematicians deal with a world of numbers. Numbers are fixed, but one can hardly classify a mathematician as having a fixed mindset. A person with a fixed mindset isn't locked in. He or she is quite capable of developing a more flexible growth mindset.

Many people who are convinced they have a fixed mindset may be living a myth. Everyone has potential, and it is that potential that can help develop what is called "creative confidence." Everyone can believe that they can create change in their environment. Even people who think they have fixed mindsets can set their minds to achieving a task they set out to do. What they can also do is go about performing a familiar task differently than they normally do.

Are you routinized? Rigid routines are creativity killers. Their single advantage is security, and their driving force is fear. People who don't take chances aren't safe at all. They will be floored the first time the unexpected happens. Those are the people who jump a mile when someone hollers or screams. Compulsive routines mute creative thinking, close minds, and feed into strengthening a fixed mindset.

No one thinks that a routine can be harmful. However, studies have shown that it can take anywhere from 10 weeks to 2½ months to break a routine. Other studies have shown that it can take anywhere from 18 to 254 days to break a routine.

The best way to do it is to make small changes to your schedule. Go to work a different way. Stop watching TV after a certain hour and read or surf the Internet. The first thing that might happen is the fact that you will lose motivation. One way in which you can combat that is to remind yourself that you're opening up your mind to new mental adventures. The other advantage is that you're creating a springboard to develop not only creativity in your thinking, but a growth mindset. Remember, too, that not everyone is purely fixed in their mindset.

It's *hard* to be different! Nurturing the motivation to change and to grow is *hard*. Developing a growth mindset is *hard*. It means that a person needs to look at their limitations and make a conscious effort to change them. Instead of seeing your shortcomings as a sentence read out in the court of your mind, limitations are growth opportunities. They aren't failures; they're learning experiences. However, you need to make a conscious daily effort to eliminate them. They are opportunities for doing something different. That isn't comfortable; it's *hard*.

Your shortcomings hold you back from achieving your full potential. There is a half-muted voice within you that whispers inside you. How is it possible to turn off the mute button?

# Chapter 4 – Active Listening

*Did You Know?*

We think at about 1000 to 3000 words per minute. We listen to about 125 to 150 words per minute. However, we're distracted about 75% of the time and remember around 20% of what we hear.

On the other hand, active listeners listen 70% of the time. They speak only about 30% of the time.

**Listening in Order to Persuade**

In Chapter 1, the topic of keywords was discussed. Keywords are essential if you are actively listening, and should you wish to persuade another person. They are utilized as a means to test whether or not you truly understand what the other person wants along with the emotions he conveys.

In Chapter 2, body language was explored. That is ancillary to an effective program of active listening.

The two aspects that are communicated to an active listener are content (through the words spoken) and emotion (through tone, facial expressions, and body behaviors).

At the end of your listening sessions, the persuasive person will have ascertained both the keywords that flowed from the content of the message, along with the accompanying emotions. *Memorize those keywords*. They will come in handy later on in the process.

At the very end of a listening session, or even at appropriate short moments while listening, the active listener **paraphrases** what the other has said; perhaps even **reframes** the issue; **acknowledges** it, and then **summarizes** it for clarification purposes.

**The Problem with Listening**

Active listening is what is called a "soft skill." That term comes from the military and means that no machinery is required to conduct the activity. The term has expanded to mean that it is a facet of social intelligence, one of the interpersonal skills we use to communicate and understand thoughts and feelings.

Have you ever noticed yourself listening to someone and preparing your response before they finish talking? Be honest. We all have. Everyone has opinions and wants to be heard. Some people may subtract themselves from listening to prepare an impressive response. That defeats the purpose of listening. The communication is from your listener; it is much more important than your "two bits," because he is the buyer, not you.

Those who spend their time listening to their own thoughts, instead of that of their buyers, are *Self-Listeners.*

---

Others, though, may blurt out a response or question before the person's finished speaking.

They are the *Interrupters.*

---

Have you ever listened... *really* listened to an interview with a politician? Many politicians will pick up on a few words in the interview, select only those issues that he or she wants to address, and talk around the issue.

They are the **Biased Listeners.**

---

How about those people who hear the first few words, and jump to the conclusion that they're not interested? Then their eyes glaze over, and their minds run into the play yard where they can think about their evening meal or plan the rest of their day.

They are the **Daydreamers.**

---

Then there are those people who move the spotlight onto themselves. They will abruptly say something like, "Oh! That reminds me of a time when I..." Then they relate a similar experience they themselves had.

They are the **Spotlight Thieves.**

---

Some people entirely miss the theme of the speaker. They zero in on details. Let's say someone is talking about their attendance at a lecture in Washington D.C. about the budget, and they ask, "Oh, was that when you lived nearby in Virginia?" They entirely missed the point.

They are the **Clueless.**

Yet, there are others who will readily give the speaker advice even though the speaker wasn't asking for that. They're very fond of saying, "You *should* do this or that."

They are the ***Advice-Givers.***

---

Many people have fallen into the trap of over-critical thinking. They often disagree with what others are saying, and do so frequently. Acceptance of the right of others to express themselves freely is vital in forming relationships. It speaks to the human being's need to exercise free speech. Some listeners subscribe to the common beliefs held by the peer group. If a speaker so much as deviates from that, some listeners will "jump down their throats" for their sin against the expected.

They are the ***Prosecutors.***

---

Avoid "why" questions. "Why" questions aren't recommended. They will put the person on the defensive. A person's fellow listeners might become uncomfortable if the speaker starts to stumble with responses and/or feels he must justify his every statement or opinion. By all means, don't stumble over your words. The real reason for a "why" question is "Why are you talking about this? Why is it important?" In that case, you have some meat. There's a reason for your talk – and that is the benefit your project or product offers.

They are the ***Combative Listeners.***

Avoid pity. If the speaker is expressing their feelings or explaining a difficult situation they confronted, do not say something to the effect like, "Oh, you *poor* thing." That invites the formation of a "mutual commiseration society," which generally attracts more people who are discontented. A list of negative complaints ensues from that. In both work and social relationships, it's toxic. What's more, it results in abandonment by others who would rather discuss more positive issues.

Those who form "pity parties" are ***Malcontents.***

### Active listening is a choice. It requires commitment and practice.

### Traits to Engage in Active Listening

1. Maintain good eye contact.
   People are more likely to expound on their topic when they feel that others are paying attention. Good eye contact shows respect for the speaker. Who wants to speak if their listeners are gazing around the room?

2. Try to glean some central issues in the person's presentation.
   This is similar to reading comprehension. People do tend to go into side discussions by giving examples of their topics. Those examples serve to support their topic. They're ancillary to the main issue or issues.

Try yourself out by listening to this 1975 interview with the former President Ronald Reagan in an interview with TV host, Johnny Carson. See if you can get a handle on the main topics discussed: https://www.youtube.com/watch?v=CNmnmdtcdcg

After you've listened, write down those main points. Go back and evaluate your comprehension skills.

3. Demonstrate non-verbally your interest in what they're saying.
   The best way to demonstrate this is to be aware of your body language. Lean forward and face the speaker. Otherwise, you're imparting the message that you're not interested and/or would rather be elsewhere. It's just plain rude!

4. Likewise, observe the non-verbal behaviors of the speaker.
   Is that person really interested in what they are saying? Does she look directly at her listeners? Does she occasionally smile? Does she fidget or appear nervous?

5. Verbally, paraphrase what the other person has said.
   You might use the techniques employed by therapists and counselors. They typically <u>paraphrase</u> the other person's words. According to the well-respected psychologist Carl Rogers, "When a person realizes he has been deeply heard, his eyes moisten. I think in some real sense he is weeping for joy. It is as though he was saying, 'Thank God somebody heard me. Someone knows what it's like to be me.'" Therapists also use this technique so that they understand the

issue correctly. Or, they might ask for clarification. Ask open-ended questions.

The poetess, Ruth Bebermeyer once said, "Words are windows or they're walls, they sentence us, or set us free. When I speak and when I hear, let the love light shine through me."

Questioning is an important skill in developing the kind of relationships you want to gain the trust of others. Salespeople always use that technique to sell an idea or a product. It is quite effective because the speaker feels you're "on their side," so to speak.

The clarification also shows concern and understanding. It's a fundamental trait of what is called <u>empathic listening</u>, meaning that you briefly step into the other's mind and try to see the issue from their eyes, rather than your own. Empathy is a characteristic by which the listener senses the fear, confusion or anger of the speaker without being sucked into it. To clarify that you understand, you might ask something like, "So, it annoys you when he says…"

The speaker may try to disguise their feelings, so you might want to "open the door" by showing that you're open to emotive expression by saying something like, "I'm sensing that you felt frustrated…angry…afraid…" and show acceptance by helping the speaker label the emotions experienced.

If the speaker is relating an event about which they may have some feelings, ask them how they felt when it happened. You want them to know that you *care* how they're feeling. The corollary to that is that you yourself need to be honest. If you're going to say you care, then *"care!"*

If the topic is informative, encourage the speaker to keep up the conversation. You might say something like, "Is that a fact?" Occasionally nod in agreement if appropriate.

6. Reduce external distractions.
   Turn off the TV and the radio. Put down your magazine and try to not take notes if possible.

7. Keep refocusing upon the speaker.
   If the speaker's subject is complex, it may be necessary to refocus your attention on the speaker.

8. Don't agree or disagree.
   The use of noncommittal words encourages a speaker to elaborate. Carl Rogers, the psychologist, calls this "unconditional positive regard." This kind of communication is non-judgmental. Being non-judgmental is the essence of active listening. Dale Carnegie has said, "Do not criticize, condemn, or complain."

If you strongly disagree, hold off your comments until the speaker is finished. Phrase your questions diplomatically, adding something like, "I'm not the world's authority on such matters...I could be wrong, but..."

9. The "Pregnant Pause"

The "Pregnant Pause" and "Pregnant-Pregnant Pause are both highly prized skills.
Don't be afraid of pauses in the conversation. Shutting up is hard to do. A person-to-person interaction isn't a telephone call, during which the listener is expected to say something once a speaker becomes silent. Everyone compulsively wants to avoid being asked, "Hello? Hello? Are you there?"

Salespeople use this technique to solicit customer responses. It works, as it usually opens the floor to questions from the customer, and increases the possibility of a sale because the listeners have time to digest and reflect upon what was presented.

The pause is also used by a speaker to elicit a response, especially when a novel idea or proposal has been made.

Studies have been performed worldwide with the "pregnant pause." English-speakers are the least comfortable with any pause of more than four seconds, while the Japanese were comfortable with silences of eight seconds!

Dr. Deborah Tannen, a linguistics professor at Georgetown University said, "As soon as you need words, there's already a failure to understand each other so you're repairing that failure by using words." However, she was quick to add, "The intention and effect of silence may be quite different." A salesperson may leave a three-second pause, while a counselor might use a five-second pause. Chinese negotiators are aware of the discomfort of Americans with the pause, so they have often used it to their advantage because it may tempt the listeners to easily make concessions.

**What to Avoid and What to Do**

In the case of a person approaching you with a problem, the usual response is to try to change their mind. It is the way you might see the situation, and your subsequent responses might be to plead, scold or encourage the other to resolve the issue the way *you* would.

However, according to the psychologist Carl Rogers, this indicates that you are looking at the situation through your own needs. It is humanly difficult to put yourself in the frame of mind of the other. Perhaps it feels intolerable to you, as you know you might not respond the way the other person would if they were left to their own resources. Yet, the truth always remains that you are *NOT* the other person. What you may permit yourself to do is to slide into a mistake sometimes made in marriages – that is when one partner tries to *change* the other.

In a verbal exchange, that would be tantamount to an insult. In other words, you would be implying that the other's viewpoint is inherently *wrong* and yours is inherently *right*.

Active listeners don't do that. They respect the personality of the other person and let them be themselves. Your function, then, is clear: you're a facilitator. You want to help the other person resolve the issue in a way that suits them and their personality.

In a supervisor-employee relationship, it is useless to present the usual trite statements like "the road to success in business is a long and difficult one, and you must be patient," or "I'm sure everything will work out OK."

For example, suppose a worker approaches the supervisor and glibly states he's finished with the drill press setup. If it was, for instance, one of his early attempts, a sensitive supervisor might ask him, "So what do you think about doing it?" He might say he never wants to do it again, or he might say he had a rough time doing it. The supervisor has now communicated the fact that he is sensitive to the worker's needs. That will also open the door for further communication. The employee appreciates that fact that his supervisor cares about him as a person and as a worker. An average boss-employee relationship has now become a good one. If that were done more often in companies, there would be far less turn-over. The employees would feel understood. What's more, many employees have ideas as to how to improve on processes in the company, and that opens the door to changing procedures. The supervisor might not agree to all the new suggestions, of course, but they might create an employee-based committee to streamline a process.

This technique also works with co-workers. When a co-worker elicits emotive reactions from a new worker, it creates a positive work relationship. However, it must represent a sincere interest. Most people are keen enough to realize whether you're simply humoring them, or you mean what you say. When you elicit the feelings of another, they will want to know your feelings as well, so personal risk is involved. In addition, the attitudes of the other person may change the way you feel about an issue.

**Mindful Listening**

Dr. Jon Kabat-Zinn was a physician at the University of Massachusetts Medical School and developed a meditative technique for the reduction of stress for his patients called the *Mindfulness Stress Reduction Program*. Kabat-Zinn had traveled to India and studied under Zen Buddhist monks, and based his methodology upon their teachings. Once the movement reached the United States, mindfulness techniques were applied to many practices, including listening. Mindful listening helps a person clear the mind sufficiently enough to assess the motives of others, as well as their desires. One can learn what is most likely to please another and draw people to you. Fortified with that information, you can influence others and become an effective and powerful leader.

---

Exercise:

Find a friend or colleague to sit down with you. Spend a minute in silence. Be very aware of your surroundings and mentally place yourself in the here-and-now.

---

> Ask the friend or colleague to speak for three minutes. The topic is up to them.
>
> Note how many times your mind wanders on to other thoughts, either related to the topic or otherwise.
>
> Answer the following questions:
> Did you feel the urge to give your partner advice?
>
> Were you thinking about something similar, or even trying to make a better, more carefully worded presentation of your own?
>
> What emotions did you experience?
>
> Then, regurgitate the content of the speaker's presentation. Let them tell you whether or not you understood the important points he or she made.
>
> Did you make any assumptions that weren't communicated to you?

In 2012, a study was conducted at Columbia University to predict how influential a person can be at work. They discovered that those who are poor listeners were considered less influential by their colleagues and supervisors in the workplace.

> The Delivery Project

Harold, a supervisor at a paper company, admitted to himself when he was reviewing the week that he had asked Amy to perform a task for him by outlining the responsibilities of the delivery department, along with a system of accountability. In a few days, she responded with a fleshed-out outline of the plan.

Upon reflection, the supervisor noted that he hadn't made much of a response. He also realized that he failed to convey any sense of confidence to the employee, nor give her any sense that would boost her self-esteem.

That, Harold realized, may have damaged his relationship with Amy and certainly didn't contribute to her motivation to do even better with her next project.

One of the reasons for that was the fact that so much is done digitally these days. That tends to dehumanize and de-legitimatize another's work. It was, after all, more than a text, an email, and a pdf of the final project.

Harold then made a personal approach and praised Amy for her work. Not only that, but he had her appointed to head up various phases of the task.

The delivery efforts made by the company streamlined the process to the point where the company was able to solicit more work and that resulted in higher profits.

It is tempting to assume that digital work is "busy work," but principles of active listening still apply. The employee didn't simply read the assignment; she read it, analyzed it, interpreted it, and carried it out in reality.

In addition to digital work, the principles of active listening are essential. For example, in a digital exchange between two workers, it's very easy to misinterpret. That occurs in social media frequently. Clarification of the issues involved are just as important as with verbal conversation, if not more so.

**Techniques Matched to the Buyers' Listening Styles**

Of course, you need to appeal to others according to their listening styles. What personality types will respond to you according to their psychological makeup? There are 3 different personality types based on listening styles.

First of all, it's paramount to assess your listeners quickly. Spend the first few minutes building a rapport with your listener. Assess whether or not you have his or her attention. Are they looking directly at you? Are their eyes darting around? Or, are you getting a stare? Are they shifting around a lot? Are they very still? Do they look intense, or do they look as if they're waiting to be entertained?

In other words, ask yourself, "What makes them tick?" "What (do you think) is the most important thing in that person's life?" Once you have a clue as to what drives that person, you'll get a general idea of their listening style.

How to Convince a People-Oriented Listener

The people-oriented listener is immensely curious about the speaker and his or her personality. You may notice that they glance at others around the room and then back at you. That's a dead giveaway. They're wondering what others are thinking about you and about them. They also want to know how the speaker thinks, so their eyes dart right back to you. They wonder what your motivations are and what their proposal or product will do to boost the listener's self-image in the eyes of others. Will it help them, as the subject, feel important? Will it be enjoyable to use your product or service? Is it helpful in attracting the interests of others? The people-oriented listener is very concerned about what others think of them. Above all, they want to be loved. They like to smile and love to be entertained and be entertaining as well. It gives them meaning.

Focus on words like "fun," "fascinating," "awesome" or "exciting." Use emotionally-charged words. Be sure to look the part! Have fun presenting! Permit yourself to get excited about your product/service. This person responds to the emotive aspects of the message. Demonstrate that you like them as a person. Compliment them, but make it sincere.

These people like spontaneity, so move on toward getting a commitment right away. Yep! That's right! These people know what they like and what they want and make quick and powerful decisions.

How to Convince the Friendly Listener

The friendly listener is other-directed, like the people-oriented listener. However, the biggest difference lies in the fact that your friendly listener is quite rational and will evaluate your product or service critically. They are intense people, and their looks can be somewhat disconcerting, but don't feel threatened by that. Therefore, be rational yourself. Point out the logic and the wisdom of using your service.

Be friendly and courteous with them. Chat with them initially, but don't overdo it, or your effort will seem too obvious. Because a person with this listening style is rational, stress that your goods are worthwhile and rewarding. You need to help them feel that they're making the right decision if they choose to buy your goods. That will not be easy to do, so use the words "right decision" at least twice in your presentation. It may take longer to convince the friendly listener to buy your product or service. Be patient and spend the time they seem to need.

<u>How to Convince the Impatient Listener</u>

These people are accustomed to making rapid decisions, but those decisions aren't impulsive. Listeners like these usually have a busy schedule, and they pack their days with value-oriented choices. They may shift around in their seat a lot, due to their impatience. You'll know by the expressions on their faces. Do they seem anxious for you to get to the heart of your discussion? Do they appear to want you to "get to the point?"

Drum up some effective, powerful words to use to describe the product or process you offer. They're not interested in you necessarily; just what purpose your product serves. They're intelligent and may interrupt you with pointed questions, so it's vital you know your product "inside-out." They also respond well to something that's quick and easy to do. They're focused on use, not appearance, nor do they care what others think about them. These are independent thinkers, and they choose their purchases carefully. However, they know what they can use and what they can't use. These people make quick decisions, so select your power words wisely.

## Online Conversations

1. <u>Focus</u>
   It is so easy to slide into an attitude of passive listening, such as that done in viewing ads or in watching a light morning program. When you're conversing online about a work project (or even a personal matter), make the effort to read what the other person said...*really read it*. Refrain from jumping to conclusions. It's foolish to conclude that you already know what a person is going to say. The other person deserves your active attention.

2. <u>Think Before Speaking</u>
   Resist responding right away. If the issue is somewhat complex, let the other person know you'll think about it and respond the following day. That will give you time to truly study the response.

3. <u>Good Questions</u>
   Formulate good questions after the person makes a statement. Pauses are OK; they tell the other person you're really considering the issue. Rather than immediately telling them what you think should be done, challenge them to present solutions. After all, you're not the "answer man." You might be pleasantly surprised by their responses.

## Active Listening Is a Skill

No one should assume that he or she is automatically an active listener. Active listening is a <u>learned</u> skill, particularly in this day and age when there is an onslaught of spoken words via

TV, podcasts, YouTube videos, Ted Talks, cell phones with text messages and voice messages, commercials. People are so easily numbed by the explosion of speech that it's almost a defense to "turn it off." That has made it all too easy to ignore the thunder of the voices.

Active listening may not be *effective* listening without practice. Your mere facial expressions will give you away every time you are or are not engaged in active listening. Others will absolutely know if you're touching base with them "where they live," so to speak. Nothing is as effective as sincerity and acceptance of the other person. You will see it immediately in their face. His or her face will "light up," as if they are silently saying, "Finally, I have found someone who truly understands who I am and where I'm coming from."

# Chapter 5 – Empowerment in Relationships

Suppose a dog approaches you. He's wagging his tail. If you reach down to pet him, he gets excited, looks up in appreciation, and even seems to be smiling. He's nearly jumping out of his skin as if you are the most interesting person he has ever met. When you speak to him, the dog doesn't have a clue what you're saying, but he's delighted to listen. What's more, he doesn't want to sell you a house or an insurance policy. He's interested in *you*. When you come home from work, he rushes to the door and acts as if he's going to jump out of his skin. He doesn't even want you to give him a treat. Your presence is sufficient. It makes you feel good. It makes you feel important, which is what Dale Carnegie cited as a vital human need as well.

Dogs don't work for a living. Before you know it, you want to give them something – food, toys, and long walks. Chickens have to lay eggs. Cows are expected to give milk. They're not particularly interested in you; they're only interested in what you can give them, like food and shelter, and they give back according to expectations. Dogs (and cats) give affection. Just affection, but it works.

You can get yourself a girlfriend, a boyfriend, and even a future spouse by showing a genuine interest in the other person. You can get more friends in a couple of months than you can in a couple of years by showing interest in people. People are interested in themselves. This is a natural human trait, without which people can't survive. When you demonstrate appreciation for others, they cannot help but respond. When performers come out on the stage, you clap. Have you ever noticed those who clap back at you? What happens? You immediately make up your mind that you're going to like their performance, even before it takes place. Magicians have the same effect on their audiences. There's a myriad of books on how to do magic, but it is the outgoing personality and the sense of humor the magician demonstrates that draws the people in to watch the act.

---

Relationships are never perfect whether they be love relationships, friendships or work relationships. We are human, and as humans, we are flawed. Unlike sales, relationships are long-term, or intended to be. Do you know your own needs? Under the shadow of emotion, in the case of a love relationship, you might underestimate your needs or sacrifice them to oblige the other "just to be nice."

Do you know the needs of the other person? No relationship – whether it be one of love and friendship or an employer-employee relationship – survives without a clear understanding of expectations and personality.

A love relationship can deceive you by substituting emotion for reasoning. Practical psychology is essential in determining success in any endeavor, especially in marriage.

## Before the Leap

Before committing yourself to a relationship, you must distance yourself from your emotions and analyze the psychological aspects of yourself and the person you are wanting a relationship with. Will you be happy? Will the other person help you fulfill your needs? As a human being, will you feel more powerful? Can you fulfill their needs? You will if you and the other have compatible needs and complementary personality types.

Below are general guidelines, followed by a technique to determine the personality type of your desired partner.

<u>General Interpersonal Guidelines</u>

### Know Yourself

If you want a satisfying relationship, you need to *know yourself* and your needs. Never lose sight of that in the emotional rush. It is you who wants to have control over the outcome of your desired relationship.

It is never good to surrender your power to another. No one person, no matter how wonderful they are, can fulfill all your needs. Your locus of control needs to come from within you. Yes, if you love the other person, you want their approval, but there are limits. You cannot fulfill all their needs either.

### Communication

Communication, of course, is essential to achieving your goal of having a meaningful relationship. Your feelings need to be expressed, as well as your needs. Time must be devoted to working toward that goal. Your relationship is a partnership, and the more balanced it is in terms of mutual fulfillment of needs, the healthier it is. A bond can be established, and more importantly maintained, only when you create opportunities for interaction. That's one of the reasons why long-distance relationships don't tend to work over the long-term.

Communication includes emails, texting, phone calls, as well as plain and simple chatting. Try to spend your evening meal telling each other something "funny" that happened during the day. Honesty is essential, but can be risky. What you want to do is to communicate the "true you" to the other, not how you want them to perceive you, because you can't keep that masquerade going on indefinitely. Think of a sales situation. If a salesperson wants to sell a product or an idea, the best approach is not to over-exaggerate or make promises that can't be fulfilled.

Explore all the traditional areas, like the other person's likes and dislikes, work, hobbies, and interests. Determine if they have the same kind of sense of humor you have.

Smile often and widely, meeting eye-to-eye. Once you do that, the other person will mimic it. If they don't, you're in trouble!

**Children**

Children are a blessing and a gift. They bring joy into a couple's life. There are, however, pitfalls in your relationships with your children. Amazingly, children have an uncanny ability to ascertain the shortcomings of each parent. If you say "no," rest assured they will rush to your partner to compare responses. Be sure to agree on disciplinary measures. That also gives children a sense of security, which is their primary need early in life.

Some parents, often mothers, spend too much time caring for the children. That harms the other partner, who suddenly feels locked out of the love from the caring parent. As soon as you can, while the children are very young, teach them that you and your partner need time for each other. Set a particular time of the day for you and your partner to be together and be firm in your resolve. In healthy relationships this works well, and the children learn respect for you and your needs. They then transfer that learning to their siblings and to others when they start dating.

**Misplaced Empowerment**

When you meet someone you really want, be sure you didn't choose them because they will meet an unmet need of your own. Another person cannot fulfill all of your own internal needs. Otherwise, you will become dependent upon the other person rather than being your own person. That will put a lot of pressure upon them, and they will recognize that you look to them to fill your own personal void. Everyone must respond to their inner voice to be all they can be, and the partner is like a team member, standing on an equal level. Having another loving person sharing a life with you brings a sense of magic and excitement.

---

<u>True Story:</u>   Distorted Relationships: The "Needy" Relationship

Maggie met Brian at a wedding. Brian was a strong person, very much in control of who he was and what he wanted in life. That's what drew Maggie to him. However, Maggie was a "needy" person. She sought him out for his personal strength. When she felt insecure, she talked to him. Brian responded by building up her confidence. She was immensely grateful to him and never ceased to compliment him on his wisdom and power. That gave him a sense of importance and he was flattered by her attention. He was able to control her; he felt empowered by her. However, that's as far as the relationship went.

In time, the relationship faltered because she couldn't meet his needs to be supportive of him in his activities or his work. Instead, she would call him at odd hours looking for his support. He would always oblige her, but she was either unwilling or unable to fill his needs. She was like the child and he was like the parent.

This was what is called a "toxic relationship." Little by little, he failed to return her phone calls and avoided seeing her.

Breakups are never comfortable in these circumstances and they are usually painful, so it is best to assess the personality type of the other person while keeping in mind the fact that it is the other's responsibility to fill your needs as well.

**Vulnerability**

Once you've entered a relationship, you're vulnerable. That's a risk, as it's important to reveal aspects of yourself. You have no idea how the other person will respond to you. Often others won't tell you what they don't like about you. That's why being able to read body language can be helpful. The individual will demonstrate their thoughts through their reaction to what you say and do.

One factor that can hamper any relationship is the fact that some people are overly concerned about how they come across to others. That will make you very unhappy in time because it's not genuine. It is a vulnerability which often leads to a long-term pre-marital relationship. One or both partners realize that if the other partner changes after marriage, it will lead to a tragic and painful break-up. The opposite is also true. Historically, short-term relationships don't work out. That's not to say they never work, however. "Love at first sight" has actually worked out very well for a number of people.

## Personality Types

If you want a particular marriage partner, more analysis should be invested in determining whether the marriage will be more successful than superficial. The hackneyed example of a man falling in love with a woman because she's beautiful is insufficient. Yet, there are situations in which that paradigm is confounded.

## Locus of Control in a Relationship

**Locus of control** is a psychological concept regarding how much control people have over the events in their lives. Those who feel that their effort and work yield either success or failure in outcomes have an internal locus of control. Those who feel that outcomes are due to luck or fate have an external locus of control. They are victims and believe that any "hiccups" in the relationship are the fault of the other person. That will lay the foundation for an unhealthy relationship.

Once the other realizes your victim status, they can (and often will) manipulate you, become argumentative or simply leave.

In all successful relationships, one partner has more control over the pace and progress of the relationship than the other. When both people in the relationship compete for strength, it lays the foundation for hostility. There needs to be at least a silent understanding between the two as to who is the leader of the couple. That doesn't mean that the traditional, old-fashioned role of the male as "king of the castle" must prevail! There are many happy marriages between two people where the female is the dominant member. So, eschew the old-time thinking that a male must be dominant. Take a look at lions. The lioness is the hunter, while the male lion is the "laid-back" member. Yes, he does protect the family, but the lioness is the more aggressive member. So is the female in a number of other animal species - hyenas, killer whales, and elephants, among others. What's more, it's OK to be a dependent male married to a dominant female. Fortunately, that has been more acceptable in the world of today.

---

The psychologists Katherine Briggs and Isabel Briggs formed a mother-daughter team who used Carl Jung's theory of personality types and developed a test to measure those types. Their test came to be applied to marriage.

There has been a lot of research using Jungian personality types in choosing a marriage partner. The following table shows the categories of personality types described by Jung and is put into a framework forming a basis for the Briggs-Meyer Type Indicator® test.

The table below is generally based upon the Briggs-Meyer test.

| Extraversion-Introversion Partnership |
| --- |
| An extrovert has an affinity toward the outside world. The external world is the source and target of their energy. They are outgoing and seek to change situations outside of themselves. They tend to guide the direction and content of a relationship. They tend to be gregarious and are comfortable at large gatherings. They can develop strong bonds with more than just one person.<br><br>An introvert, on the other hand, draws their strength from within. They prefer relationships with one or two other people or one or two at a time. Large parties tend to turn them off. In a marriage, they tend to be wholly devoted to the other person. |
| **Sensing-Intuition (S/N) Partnership** |
| The sensing personality type will derive his or her information from the external world of facts and beliefs.<br><br>The intuitive person will derive information from within themselves. That information tends to come from his or her reaction to what is seen in the outside world. It is emotive, that is, tends to come from feelings. They will make decisions based on how they *feel*. |
| **Thinking-Feeling Partnership** |
| Thinking means that a person will make decisions based upon empirical observation, that is, upon what he or she sees in the external world. He or she is more "matter-of-fact" in their decisions.<br><br>The Felling partner tends to be more imaginative in their responses. They are more creative. Their assessments are based |

upon how they feel and how others feel. They tend to be more compassionate and understanding.

| Judging-Perceiving Partnership |
|---|
| Judging has to do with how a person processes the information they receive. They will then act upon what they *think* they should do. They are logical. They are organized.<br><br>An intuitive person will base his or her decisions upon what they feel within themselves, rather than what they externally observe. As opposed to being organized, "Perceivers" are more flexible and open-ended. |

## Extraversion-Introversion and Marriage Compatibility

A happily married man used to remark to his wife, "I loved you first," to which his wife would quip, "Yes, but I love you more!" He was the extrovert in the relationship, and she was the introvert. The marriage was rewarding because they balanced each other well. The husband *controlled* the relationship, and the wife willingly *accepted* him in that role. However, if the dominant partner excludes or ignores his or her partner, it can threaten a relationship. Or, on the other hand, the introverted partner can become overwhelmed because of the strong need the extrovert has for socializing.

The opposite case, that is, when the woman is dominant or extroverted and the male is retiring and introverted, defies the old-fashioned notion that the male must be the dominant one. In today's society, though, a more liberal view of such stereotyping is thankfully possible.

Marriages between extroverts and introverts are common, in that the introvert sees the extrovert as completing his or her imbalance. These people as partners don't compete for center stage. After the initial sparks have died out, though, conflict can occur, so moderation is important. The extroverted partner needs to be considerate of his or her opposite and give their introverted partner time alone to think. Success in this marital combination also depends upon the other factors present, such as the commonality in Jung's Personality factors of Sensing-Intuition, Thinking-Feeling, and Judging-Perceiving.

The introverted partner also needs to guard against jealousy if the extrovert befriends a person of the opposite sex in the case of a heterogeneous relationship. With homosexuals, of course, a threat might be seen in a friendship with a person of the same sex. The introvert must allow the extrovert to socialize with others. Yes, there is a risk in doing so. In all relationships, there is risk. Allowing an extroverted partner to be him or herself can keep an introvert from continually focusing inward. It's a healthy alternative and will prevent one from becoming too self-centered.

As with all personality types, recognition of the needs of the other is paramount.

Sensing-Intuition and Marriage Compatibility

In a 1981 study, Isabel Briggs Meyer and other researchers discovered that if the two partners are similar in Sensing and Intuition, compatibility is more likely to develop. They tend to view the world in the same way.

When one is more sensing than intuitive, he or she will tend to be more practical. The intuitive type will be more driven by idealism and that may create unrealistic expectations. For example, the sensing individual may fail to see that a partner is lonely or depressed and fail to satisfy the other's need for companionship. In a family get-together, one individual may be more interested in texting his or her friends than in conversing with relatives. That happens all too often in today's world of excessive conversation.

Sensing people judge situations through the senses; that is, they draw inferences from the tangible and the provable. Intuitive people notice the implications. "What does that *really* mean? Why did the person say that?" Sensing people are empiricists. They judge by facts. Intuitive people can make "leaps" in judgment, but sensing people only make decisions and judgments based on the tangible, as happens in a courtroom.

*Note- In the studies by Meyer Briggs®, the acronym, "S/N" has been used to refer to the Sensing-Intuitive personality type.

<u>Thinking-Feeling and Marriage Compatibility</u>

When two partners have feeling preferences in common, it was discovered that they are usually more compatible. In fact, it was discovered through clinical studies that people who grant importance to the depth of their feelings over the cold logic of thought can overcome personality differences in other areas. That makes sense, as the "feelers" invest more psychic energy into the relationship.

When there are differences, that is, a "Thinking" personality type and a "Feeling" personality type, the two will differ in terms of decision-making. The thinking person will make a decision based upon the objective consideration of logic, facts, and truisms. The feeling person will make decisions based upon a people-oriented approach. For instance, they will reflect upon another's reaction to a tentative decision before flying into action. The thinker might find that foolish, because another person's possible negative reaction may be predicted.

Thinkers need to avoid criticism, while feelers need to realize that the other's opinion might be the correct one.

## Judging-Perceiving and Marriage Compatibility

"Judgers" tend to have a sense of organization, while perceivers want more freedom in their lives. Perceivers may tend to be sloppy, while their opposites can be driven half-crazy by their flexible view of things. While there is a reward in a sense of organization, a judger can be rigid. Perceivers also tend to procrastinate. "That's on my 'list of things to do," they often say. Procrastination is used as a means to reduce stress; manifesting is the strategy of putting off an unpleasant task at least until one is ready.

The truth of the matter is the fact that there may actually be some advantage to waiting until one is ready to deal with difficult tasks. The judger will do the unpleasant tasks first. "I'll do that first," they will say, "to get it over with." Perceivers all too often start projects but never finish them. A successful relationship in that regard can sometimes be accomplished if the judger finishes what the other person started. The challenge, of course, is to avoid repressing resentment and internalizing anger. That is where a sense of humor helps one out.

Studies have shown that differences in this area brought out more problems in a relationship than would be anticipated. When the judger insisted that his or her partner keep in tune with the program, so to speak, it angered the perceiver as they felt controlled.

It is very difficult for the judger to be patient with the perceiver. Both need to work together to make the relationship work. Perceivers can help judgers relax and "go with the flow."

**Putting your Power into Work Relationships**

*"There is only one way under high heaven to get anybody to do anything. Did you ever stop to think of that? Yes, just one way. And that is by making the other person want to do it."* – Dale Carnegie

Healthy relationships at work bring job satisfaction, raise your quality of life, and facilitate teamwork. You actually spend more time with your work colleagues than you do with your own families. Yet, it takes time to build these relationships and time to learn how to control them to your advantage. Like meeting people at a party, these relationships start by being superficial. It is inevitable and it is recommended that you share something personal with your colleagues. This builds trust. Trust is an essential bond that will help you gain a level of control over the direction of any project you want to get your staff to fulfill. Being genuine and appreciative is an important way to form a connection between you and those who work for or with you. As with any relationship, the needs of the other person are crucial. Ask yourself "What does that person need right now?"

The world is loaded with self-seeking people. Those of you who can put yourselves in the place of the other person and see a project from their point of view have a tremendous advantage. You can point out the factors that will be advantageous for both of you at the completion of the other person's tasks Is this manipulation? Yes and no. It resembles a negotiation in that each side achieves something, although they may have to make a sacrifice in doing so. It is a "win-win" relationship.

---

<u>True Story:</u>    The Making of a Salesman

In an Eastern U.S. city, a man by the name of George applied as a worker on an assembly line and was hired by Merrick, the personnel manager. In time, Merrick noted George's personality and how he communicated with his co-workers. They liked George. He also imparted a sense of reliability and others trusted him. When questions arose on the line, others would ask him for his opinion. Besides, he always filled in for others when they had to take breaks. Occasionally, George would make suggestions to streamline the process, and was very persuasive. When his supervisor rejected George's suggestions, he was never dismayed or annoyed. He accepted it.

Merrick liked George's manner and his persuasive style, and felt he would be a fantastic salesman. George had very little education and absolutely no experience in sales. Now, how was Merrick going to get George to work for him in sales? George would, no doubt, feel insecure about such a change.

Before Merrick called George to his office, he prepared a few jokes. He also actually practiced smiling. As George was walking up the hallway toward Merrick's office, Merrick stood up, walked toward George, smiled, and shook his hand. He offered George some coffee and cookies.

Merrick then asked George if he'd like to make more money at the company. Sure! However, as soon as Merrick proposed the idea that George might try his hand at sales, panic set in. George's eyes glazed over and he lapsed into a stare. Merrick waved his hands at George and quipped, "Earth to George! Earth to George! I didn't bring you in here to terrify you," Merrick remarked with a smile.

Merrick pointed out George's strengths to him. He noted how others responded to him. Merrick expressed his appreciation for George's work. The incentive in raising his salary and adding on commissions to that wasn't enough. Merrick had to negotiate. He promised that George would still get his pension and his benefits if the new position didn't pan out.

George had a whole string of objections, much like the objections that potential customers present to a salesman. Merrick was in the curious position of selling the job to his employee!

There are proven steps to be taken to make a positive answer more likely.

- Listen
  Listen carefully to the person, holding eye-to-eye contact. Respond to each one thoughtfully and sincerely. Point out the benefits.
- Understand

Not everyone expresses themselves well. Be sure you understand the objections and address them accordingly. Be sympathetic and give the other the right to feel as he does.

- Respond

  Respond to each of the objections thoughtfully and one at a time. If he is willing to give the new course a try, move ahead. Don't let any time lapse, so he won't change his mind.

- Confirm

  This is the call to action: "If you're ready to make the move, I'll speak with your supervisor and he can make the arrangements. In the meantime, I'll set you up with a small office and acquaint you with the sales route. One of our other salesmen can explain all the ropes."

The strategy worked. George became one of the most successful and profitable salesmen in the entire company and was put in charge of national sales.

# Chapter 6 – The Crack in the Liberty Bell

The Liberty Bell is a symbol of American Independence. It is located at Independence Hall in Philadelphia, Pennsylvania, which was made the capital of the USA in 1752, when its manufacture was commissioned. It is believed that the Liberty Bell was first rung on July 8, 1776, during the reading of the Declaration of Independence. Contrary to popular opinion, it wasn't ready to be rung on July 4th, the official date of America's independence. Daily life often brings delays.

The cause of the appearance of the infamous crack in the Liberty Bell is unknown. Also unknown is when the crack first formed. Evidence of the crack started to show in the 19th Century, not the 18th Century when it was first rung.

Americans were disappointed, so the bell was recast by the Whitechapel Foundry, the same foundry that manufactured it initially. It arrived in Philadelphia in 1752. All did not go well. Isaac Norris, the Speaker of the House of the Provincial Assembly in Philadelphia, was shocked when the rim of the newly cast bell cracked upon its first ringing!

Those who were more superstitious then felt that the bell should be cast in America. So, John Pass and John Stowe offered to do it at their Mount Holly Foundry in New Jersey. When rung, the bell did not break, but "earwitnesses" indicated it sounded like two coal shuttles banging together! So, the bell was recast yet again! Norris didn't particularly like the sound of the new bell. It had a tenor ring and lacked the gravitas people would expect of the symbol of American liberty. At that point, everyone gave up, so they decided to keep both bells. The year was now 1754 – 22 years from the date of the Declaration of Independence.

Why didn't they recast it yet again?

Because they accepted the fact that the bell was *flawed*. That is also true of the human condition.

## We Are Flawed!

When someone embarks upon a project or an activity, they don't expect to fail. They expect to succeed. That's healthy. However, like the manufacture of the Liberty Bell, the outcome isn't always what's anticipated.

Acceptance of failure is an uncomfortable but inevitable part of life. What's more, it's familiar. It happened when you were an infant and dropped your bottle on the floor for the first time. We aren't born into this world in a perfect condition, but we seem to think we are, for reasons beyond comprehension.

The truth of imperfection started when everyone was young. Every child has been raised with a list of "Don'ts:"

"Don't touch the stove!"

"Don't play with the scissors!"

"Don't run in the house!"

So, what happens when Johnny overlooks his mother's advice? Johnny races through the house, runs into the bathroom, slips, falls, and slams his head into the toilet bowl! Johnny didn't plan on doing that, and it's a real surprise when it happens. He believed that pain only happens to other people, like his pesky little brother!

Now, what may happen if Johnny heeds his mother's advice? He walks through the house, walks into the bathroom, slips on a sliver of wet soap, falls, and slams his head into the toilet bowl anyway! Of course, it doesn't happen every time, but still may happen.

Such things happen to human beings, giving rise to the truism: ***We are flawed.***

### And You?

What's that you said? You're flawed, too? Flawed like the rest of us?

As human beings, we're hard-wired to like ourselves – that's why! Then life blows in like an intemperate wind and bats you around a bit. If you fall, you'll get back up again. Why? Because you're alive and well, and a LOT stronger than you thought you were. Surely, there are other qualities you have, but you've put them down, through a sense of false modesty. What's more, you've overlooked contributions you can make and have made. You have skills you can use, and you have accomplishments to celebrate.

What would happen if ordinary people stopped making their own contributions to society for just a few days? The whole world would come to a screeching halt! You don't have to be a celebrity to make your personal contributions to society. You don't have to be an important government official. You don't have to be rich and famous. So, remind yourself that the world could stop without you and everyone else. Remind yourself that if others can grow and change, so can you. You have within you the amazing ability to become even better than you were.

Surely, in life, you've come across spiteful hate-filled people, and you know you're not one of them. So, what about you? What are you grateful for? Take some time and make a list. Yes, you will underestimate your contributions and you will underestimate things that deserve your gratitude.

Look at yourself in the mirror. The first thing you'll notice are your imperfections. Look beyond that and stare deeply into the reflection of your eyes. See yourself for all your positives. They are there in the depth of your soul. Love what you see. You had no problem doing that when you were a child. Children are naturally honest with themselves. Reawaken that.

**"I Can't."**

"I can't" is the most damaging statement in any language. If you're so fond of piping up with "I can't," why can't you? Do you have a plausible reason? Do you feel hopelessly outnumbered like a soldier in a war? Convincing someone of something isn't a war. Surrendering to the negative assertion, "I can't," will only start an internal argument – you vs. you. Avoid creating a war in yourself. Trust yourself enough to say, "I can," because you *can*. It may just be a case of learning how to. The more negatives that you nibble for your cognitive lunch will give you nausea. Suppress the negatives, and develop positive thoughts about yourself. That isn't easy, it's challenging. Others have done it before you. So can you.

Your listeners aren't your enemies. You like yourself, so extend that same courtesy to them. LIKE your listeners. They are interested in listening to 'lil' ol' you'. Imagine that! You really *are* worth your salt, after all.

Your listeners aren't forming a firing squad. They will have questions, though, not because they want to defeat you; they're curious about your offer. That's a good sign! You have their interest. In addition, they're providing you with the clues you need to sell your project or product. You now have a tremendous advantage, and they handed it to you for free!

Smile, even when you don't feel up to it. Look at your smile in the mirror. Do you look happy? Do you look silly? Does your expression make you giggle? Smiling can kick in a few of those natural endorphins. So, let your body teach your mind.

You're no rock-solid narcissist who's deluded enough to think he can talk anybody into anything. In fact, narcissists really can't do that very well anyway, and will quit when confronted, or have a knock-down-drag-down fight with the people they want to convince.

**Handling Failure**

The 20th Century psychologist, Albert Ellis, stated that people have developed beliefs about themselves he labeled "irrational." When those beliefs are contradicted, people are surprised. He presented a list of eleven of the most common irrational beliefs:

> *(Violin music begins…)*
> 1. **"I need love and approval** from those around me."

2. "To be valuable, I **have to achieve everything** that I set out to do."
3. "**Bad people must be punished** for their bad actions."
4. "It is horrible and **catastrophic** that things are not the way I want or desire, do not go that way, or do not turn out that way."
5. "Human unhappiness finds its origin in **external causes** and I cannot do anything or almost anything, to avoid or control the pain and suffering it causes me."
6. "**I have to constantly think** that the worst can happen."
7. "It is easier to **avoid** than to face responsibilities and problems in life."
8. "**We have to have someone stronger to trust in.**"
9. "**My past is determinant of my present and future.**"
10. "I **have to constantly worry** about other peoples' problems."
11. "Every problem has a right solution, and it is a **catastrophe** if I do not find it."

## Confusing Cognition with Emotion

Considering the information above, the person has made one cognitive error after another. If you fail to entice people to enlist in your cause, or you fail to sell them your product or service, you will **feel** bad. The immediate human reaction to failure is emotional, not cognitive. What Ellis has listed above are beliefs…that is, thoughts.

> Re: #1- **"I need love and approval** from those around me."

This is the only item that relates to feelings. Yes, every human being needs the esteem of others. As to whether or not you need love and approval from those *around you* - that may be unrealistic. Regardless of whether you're religious or not, there is great wisdom in the Bible. Jesus Christ once said, "A prophet has no honor in his own country" (John 4:44). If the people around you don't approve of you, it doesn't mean no one *else* in the world approves of you.

The remainder of Ellis's irrational beliefs represents cognitive conclusions. They are irrational because they don't address the issue.

> Re: #2- "To be valuable, I **have to achieve everything** that I set out to do."

This is a <u>thought</u>, a belief in a falsehood. *No one* has achieved everything they set out to do.

> Re: #3- "**Bad people must be punished** for their bad actions."

This, too, is a <u>thought,</u> and it places the blame on others.

> Re: #4- "It is horrible and **catastrophic** that things are not the way I want or desire, do not go that way, or do not turn out that way."

This is a <u>thought</u>. It is a falsehood, as the conclusion is all-encompassing. What's more, it leaves no room for change.

> Re: #5- "Human unhappiness finds its origin in **external causes** and I cannot do anything or almost anything, to avoid or control the pain and suffering it causes me."

This is a <u>thought</u>. It is a falsehood as it places the blame elsewhere and on to something non-specific.

> Re: #6- **"I have to constantly think** that the worst can happen."

This is, again, a <u>thought</u>. It also triggers obsession…that is, even more thoughts.

> Re: #7- "It is easier to **avoid** than to face responsibilities and problems in life."

This is a <u>thought</u>, which results in inaction.

> Re: #8- **"We have to have someone stronger to trust in."**

This is a <u>thought</u>. The statement of a need is reminiscent of a child's need for his or her mother!

> Re: #9- **"My past is determinant of my present and future."**

This is a <u>thought</u> based on a falsehood.

> Re: #10- "I **have to constantly worry** about other people's problems."

This is a <u>thought</u>. Like #6, it also triggers obsession.

Re: #11- "Every problem has a right solution, and it is a **catastrophe** if I do not find it."

This is a <u>thought.</u> Like #4, it is all-encompassing.

You had a project. You carefully researched it, formulated it, recorded it, practiced your presentation, secured a stage, a room, or a setting to present the project. If it didn't go over well, you will feel bad about it. What you are feeling are "growing pains." **So, permit yourself to feel bad about it. *IT'S OK TO FEEL!***

Some people waste too much energy on rumination. Then the failure carves itself ever deeper and deeper into one's consciousness. It is the maladaptive psychological coping mechanism. Obsession will lead its practitioner to a grinding halt. How does one dodge the rumination? By setting a time limit on the feeling, changing the topic, and developing alternatives.

Telling yourself that the blame lies outside of yourself, on circumstances, or on other people are excuses. The maladaptive coping strategy employed here is called "projection." It is you who needs to accept the responsibility for the failure. That's sufficient.

Assuming that failure is disastrous is irrational. You won't be the first to fail, and you won't be the last.

Telling yourself that you have to constantly worry about your failure is masochistic – likewise maladaptive. What would happen if you stopped worrying? Yes, you might recover. Isn't that OK?

You had an idea. If you feel you need someone stronger, you fail to give yourself the credit you deserve for having the idea in the first place. All your idea might need is a modification or a different target audience.

Some feel that the past determines your present and future. If a person believes that, they are denying the existence of change and growth. Chapter 3 indicated first of all, that a person with a fixed mindset isn't totally immersed in the fixed mindset. They have elements of both the fixed and the growth mindset. That chapter also provided some tips as to how to increase one's growth mindset and bring about change and progress.

**The Role Models**

According to Dale Carnegie, "Most of the important things in the world have been accomplished by people who have kept on trying when there seemed to be no hope at all."

Below is a list of famous people who failed, not only on their first attempt but on many attempts:

Oprah Winfrey

Walt Disney

Stephen King

Winston Churchill

Antoine Sarokian

Successful people fail regularly, but win if they persist. Take, for example, the story of Skip.

<u>True Story:</u>        Skip the Dancer

Skip's passion was ballet dancing. He had attended classes since he was a child. Skip was a charmer, and his colleagues loved him dearly. He was an avid runner, and the neighbors daily saw him outside running block after block. He went through bouts of pain along with all the sore muscle aches that accompany the pursuit. When it came time to audition, he loaded his backpack. He would then go to New York City with his editions of *Variety* and other trade magazines advertising casting calls. Skip didn't have much money, and neither did his friends, so they crashed at dingy hotels throughout the city.

Early in the mornings, the rooms emptied as the harried potential actors and dancers raced out and grabbed the buses and subways throughout the city. In the evening, they all rushed out to fill in as waitresses, busboys, and waiters at the city's restaurants. Skip sang at the tables and literally danced from one table to another. By the end of the day, he and his companions were hungry and exhausted but watched their cell phones waiting, waiting for calls before falling to sleep. Skip spent many, many summers doing that. Occasionally, Skip would go for a stint on local shows that unfortunately closed after a week or so. Then came September and he had to go back to school. "Why don't you give it up?" his brother asked him on one occasion. Skip couldn't. He was absorbed in his desire to dance.

One summer, Skip didn't show up at the dingy hotels. His friends called incessantly but got no response. Everyone was concerned. Skip was truly missed and missing.

> Then, on a rainy Saturday afternoon, a call came into one of his buddies. Skip was shouting, as he could hardly be heard. "Where have you been?" his buddy shouted into his phone.
>
> "Greece! We've been touring the world! I linked up with (name withheld). I'm in the dance troupe. I'll see you on Broadway next year!" It took perseverance and determination.

**It's OK to keep trying. Never let go of your dream and *DARE TO BE PERSISTENT IN FOLLOWING YOUR DREAM!***

Instead of obsessing on failure, obsess on being persistent.

## Try, Try Again

Mother Theresa was famous for her work with lepers in India, of which there were many. Someone once asked her how she could ever hope to take care of all of them. Quietly, she answered, "One leper at a time." That's a lesson on how to conquer the fear of failure.

Her solution to what seemed to be an insurmountable task was simple and to the point. We all have "snakes" rolling around in our heads. Failure has a nasty way of bringing *all* those nasty and venomous snakes to the forefront all at once. It is your challenge to narrow the number of snakes and take them on one at a time. Start with a stepwise strategy.

Reframe your mindset. Review your project, look for ways to improve it. Never fear making modifications to your project. Thomas Edison once said, "I have not failed. I've just found

10,000 ways that won't work." Henry Ford has said, "The only real mistake is the one from which we learn nothing."

Edison tried using the carbonized filaments of every plant imaginable – flax, bamboo, cedar, hickory, boxwood, bay wood and had tested no fewer than 6,000 plant species. Then he tried carbonized cotton and the light bulb glowed orange for fifteen straight hours! That became his famous Patent # 223,898. Every failure is a learning experience. (Note: Today the filaments are made of tungsten.)

Even when working on a simple project, objectively analyze **not why** it went wrong, **but what** went wrong. Assuming you've accepted the fact that you felt bad after the failure, and given yourself sufficient time to recover, it's time to move on to the next step. Brainstorming with your trusted colleagues will help. Never, never ask them to find something wrong. When you do that, everyone will find something to criticize. Instead, make it an open-ended question. Focus on the more objective considerations – that is, the "what's" as opposed to the "who." Failure isn't personal, although your initial emotional reaction will be a personal one.

1) Content
   If you were selling a facial lotion, brainstorm for words related to the product. For example, words like so-o-o-o-thing, cre-e-e-e-emy, smo-o-o-o-o-o-th, co-o-o-o-l. Drag out the vowels that will hypnotically convey both the meaning and the feeling of the words.
2) Strategy
   In the case of the facial lotion, develop a list of features such as gently scented, long-lasting, and nourishing due to the addition of natural vegetable ingredients.

3) Purpose
   To make you feel refreshed, clean, and protected from harsh sun and wind.
4) Cosmetics
   This would be a photo of the product. Enhancement is allowable as long as it's a color-correction or something that will truly resemble the packaging you designed. Websites may distort color to some extent because it shows the difference between RGB (based on light) and CMYK (based on pigment) color coding.

**Failure Is Never a Catastrophe**

As said earlier, failure is a learning experience. It's not the end of the world. Everyone fails once in a while, or perhaps they fail a lot, as Edison did. That doesn't mean that it will always happen; you need to make eliminations. It's better to look upon failure as a stepping stone. Like Carnegie suggested, keep trying. Don't try to forget your mistakes; learn from them. It's never healthy to obsess or worry about failure. Once you are successful, you will appreciate its value and it will motivate you to do it again and again.

Chapter 3 addresses how to develop the growth mindset. Those who have a growth mindset will have an easier time dealing with failure because they're more flexible and open to change.

**Fire Ferguson!**

Jerry Weintraub was the manager for John Denver, the hit singer. In 2011, Denver had a list of complaints about how

Weintraub and his company were handling his career. When Weintraub sat down with Denver to discuss the complaints, Weintraub addressed all the problems and corrected them. When Denver and he met again, Denver was delighted. Then Denver asked Weintraub what he did to correct all those issues.

"All of those problems were the fault of my man, Ferguson. So, I fired Ferguson."

Suddenly, Denver realized it was around Christmas time, so he appealed to Weintraub for understanding and mercy.

"OK, then," responded Weintraub. "I'll put him elsewhere in the company. There won't be any more problems with your issue." Denver felt satisfied.

The truth of the matter was the fact that ***there never was a Ferguson!***

Ferguson was what's called a "straw man" – an imagined target who's easier to defeat than the reality. It's only human to look toward someone or something else to rationalize a failure. That isn't productive. It's important that you take the responsibility, but it's futile to flog yourself.

Overcoming failure isn't easy. It's difficult. Give yourself credit for attempting to face failure and deal with it constructively.

Studies have shown that women tend to take a failure more personally than men. In a recent study involving the development of a technological program, evidence revealed that men tend to project the blame on technical occurrences, too many error messages, and overly zealous privacy protections. The women blamed it on their shortcomings, assuming it meant they were technologically stunted. Neither gender was accurate in their assessments. The failure lay in the "what" of the event, not the "who."

Self-blame comes in many disguises. If you're excessively concerned about what others will think, you've revealed that your self-image depends upon "the Great They." "The Great They" are the nameless, faceless thousands who sit in an invisible court of judgment ready to pounce upon you with a verdict. "The Great They" could be your mother or your father or a teacher you hated in the second grade. "The Great They" is what is called the Superego – a personality component that acts as a self-critical conscience.

**Beginner's Luck and the Gambler's Fallacy**

Carol Dweck, whose themes were the fixed and growth mindset, said that people with a fixed mindset "believe that talent alone creates success – not effort." If luck alone created success, then every gambler would either be perpetually a winner or a loser. The outcome would be preset. Beginner's luck would be a permanent condition.

The Gambler's Fallacy, first termed such by the Nobel Prize winning behavioral economists, Daniel Kahneman, and Amos Tversky, is a cognitive bias by which its subject believes that if an event appears to occur more frequently than might be expected, it's more likely to reoccur in the future (or vice-versa). If a coin toss ended up on "heads" twice in a row, a person may be convinced that it will land on "tails" next. This is a fallacy because each throw is independent of the other. The odds are exactly the same with each throw.

If you depend upon talent alone or luck alone to lead to success, that's like spinning a roulette wheel. The spin of the wheel may or *MAY NOT* lead to success. Warren Buffett, the multi-millionaire investor, bought 415 million shares in a UK grocery firm, Tesco, in 2012. He lost $444 million when he was forced to sell his stocks. Buffett, of course, is one of the wisest investors in the market. However, talent and luck account for a lot of the unpredictability of the stock market.

You cannot assume, then, that prior failures will lead to more in the future. Likewise, you cannot assume that – if you're successful – you can repeat it in the future. Life is like a chess game, not tic-tac-toe.

**Forgiveness**

The Superego serves a useful purpose if it prevents you from doing far too risky things like skiing down the expert's slope when you're just a beginner. Some superegos are scolding, frowning old hags that will shelter you like the womb. If you're overly cautious, your Superego can practically do you in, if you let it. Everyone can squelch the old hag inside of them. Hush! No one is looking. You *are allowed* to forgive yourself if you fail. Believe that and it will be so.

What's more important, you can learn something from failure if you're humble enough to admit it happened. Even if you have a fixed mindset, you cannot stop the clock, so you will inevitably change in time.

**Your Friend**

A useful technique you might like to use is to ask yourself what you would tell a friend if they failed to try to do the kind of project you did. This is harder to do if you don't have a history of having failed. Even the toughest of people would still have difficulty doing that.

**The Wisdom and the Witless**

Who do you think said: "A person who never made a mistake never tried anything new"? ...*Albert Einstein!*

There are, unfortunately, some people who will go to extraordinary means to avoid failure. They are the witless ones who spend their days walking in their own shadows. It is as if they feel that's where they belong. They try to avoid feeling failure by feeling nothing at all. They avoid life.

Read an excerpt from a poem by T.S. Eliot:

> "Between the idea
> And the reality
> Between the motion
> And the act
> Falls the shadow
>     *Life is very long.*
> Between the desire
> And the spasm
> Between the potency
> And the existence
> Between the essence

> And the descent
> Falls the shadow."

The first two lines of Eliot's poem, *The Hollow Men,* are very revealing, as they say a lot about the people who are content with spending their lives in the shadow, living their lives avoiding failure – *"We are the hollow men; we are the stuffed men. Leaning together, headpieces full of straw. Alas!"*

That is what happens to people who have never tried.

# Chapter 7 – Hypnosis and Influence

## Hypnosis in Sales

Neurolinguistic programming is a process by which individuals analyze strategies engaged by successful people and instill those strategies into their own lives. This process has been successfully used in sales and marketing. The message, the product or the service is motivated or propelled by a person who can 1) grab the attention of a listener, 2) harness and focus it, and 3) suggest that the listener perform a particular action. The outcome is simple: the listener will achieve some benefit and feel better for having acted.

If the speaker is selling an idea, the outcome might be that the listener will feel the success that the speaker conveyed. They have come to believe in the product, the service or the cause. Then they become one of the many happy customers who own the product or philosophy and will be likewise successful.

According to the magazine, *Selling Power: Success Strategies for Sales Management*, "Neurolinguistic Programming techniques were actually derived from the field of indirect or direct conversational hypnosis." Neurolinguistic programming is a time-tested technique created in the 1970s by Richard Bandler and John Grinder at the University of California. When applied to sales, it is quite effective. A seller first achieves a rapport from his or her listeners and then encourages the listeners to speak about their dreams, their wishes, and their own beliefs. People make decisions based not merely on facts, but on their beliefs and emotions. Those beliefs and emotions are evoked by the use of words – that is, linguistics.

It is your goal to persuade your listener that, by adopting your procedure, your service or your product, a customer will feel better by fulfilling that dream or belief they have within themselves. The Neurolinguistic techniques employ verbal patterns that are based on cognitive processes, meaning the imparting of facts that will awaken an emotion followed by a decision.

**Steps: The Power of Suggestion**

1. As a promoter or salesperson, convince yourself of the worth and the value of your service. Rekindle the interest you had when you first embarked with your idea. Cast away any negativity like "We're in a recession." In other words, mesmerize yourself into believing that <u>what you have</u> to offer is <u>valuable</u>. In other words, sell yourself to yourself!
2. Recall how excited you were when you conceived the idea. Give yourself credit for that because you deserve it. Surely, there was and still is value in the idea or product. Yes, perhaps you might want to reframe it, but there is value there. If you feel good, so will your listeners. It's contagious.
3. Look for what other people <u>dream</u> about, believe in or want in their lives. It could be something as mundane as making their lives easier and more pleasant.
4. Use vivid words or imagery in your conversation. Paint a picture of the person's environment which brings about a sense of relaxation, peace, and success. Ask him or her to tell you about a pleasing buying

experience they've had in the past. The person will then mesmerize themselves by reliving <u>a pleasurable</u> buying experience. Induce them to tell you about their thinking process when deciding to buy the service or product.

5. Restate in their words what the person has said. <u>Repetition</u> fosters reinforcement. In Chapter 4, it was suggested that you paraphrase what the other person has said, which is fine, too. Successful sales are the main reason why TV commercials are repetitive. The message becomes part of the listener's environment. It becomes comfortable. It becomes familiar, like a friend.

6. Also, in Chapter 4, the practice of "mirroring" was discussed. That means that you imitate the body language of your listener. You subtly <u>remind them they like you</u>, and that you are like them. They will identify you as a friend, an equal, and a colleague. Such actions bring about trust, and do so secretly. You will be speaking to the other person's subconscious mind, which is what is done in hypnosis.

7. Again,<u> repeat</u> the same keywords that the listener used as they told you their stories of successful purchases or services in the past.

8. In this chapter, the story of the successful salesman, Guy, relates the fact that others had purchased the product and "were delighted." He also told the potential customer that he owned such a product. You can elaborate on such stories and paint vivid pictures of using the product or service. That is likewise mesmerizing as it <u>evokes visual imaging</u> by the listener of pleasurable experiences.

9. Use a <u>soothing</u> voice– one that is deeper rather than higher in pitch. It resonates in the abdomen. It is slow and deliberate. Be sure there are inflections. Monotones bring about boredom.
10. Don't forget to intersperse your presentation with the names of your customers, if possible. Remember Dale Carnegie's adage, "A person's name is to that person, the sweetest most important sound in any language."
11. Use intraverbal suggestions. An intraverbal suggestion is done by using certain inflections in your voice. For example, "Think about how <u>e-e-e-easy</u> this will be for you." Those inflections bring about feelings of happiness and pleasure. Try that with the keywords your customer used repetitively.
12. Everyone has a "sales pitch." Of course, you need one to fall back on. However, there is a serious pitfall here. Look upon your approach as a personal interaction. Make it "other-directed."

    Adjust your focus differently. The person is not a "customer." He or she is not a "sale." A person is a *person*. Decide that you *like* that person. He or she had a need and you're going to <u>help him or her</u> as best you can. So, by all means, chat with the person briefly. Use a handshake and a genuine smile.
13. Predict <u>how happy the person will feel</u> if they enroll in your service or purchase your product.
14. Some people are defensive when approaching a salesperson. Some come in convinced that they're going to be deceived or ripped off. While you are doing your product demonstration or talking about the highlights of your proposal, they may interrupt and ask you, "How much does it cost?"

**Use a magician's trick called <u>redirection</u>. No, don't hide the price of your service or product. But as a way to elicit more information about the person's needs, you might answer such a question by saying, "Well it starts at about $50..." then interrupt yourself with a question like, "you must have a good reason for asking that, so what is your concern?" That will encourage the person to give you more information, like limitations in budget, or other bad experiences they've had in the past.**

It is also useful when you notice that your listener's attention is wandering. Another technique that helps is a quick movement or bringing both of your hands in a particular direction as if you're introducing someone to an audience. One salesman used to drop his computer tablet and it worked like magic.

15. Subtle eye movements will tell you whether the listener is telling you the truth or otherwise. If a person looks to the left, they are conjuring up images about your presentation or your product. They're thinking. <u>Capture their attention</u> by asking them what they're thinking. That can be very informative. Quick! Grab their attention by telling them to imagine what it would be like owning the product you're selling. They'll be surprised you can "read their minds." Or, you can use a more directive oppositional approach, by asking them to imagine how they would feel *without* having the benefit your product or service could provide.

16. Believe it or not, staring at a person may help them jump the last hurdle and commit themselves to the purchase of a product or process. You've all heard

about people with a "hypnotic stare." Yes, it is risky, but it can drive a person to make the decision. No need to sound too forceful, but you can ask this question: "So what do you think? It's certainly worth it, isn't it?" Again, focus your eyes just above the bridge of their nose.

The words below were used in the twelve points. **Every one of them is a suggestion that sets up a desirable outcome.** A person is led to, is coaxed to think they will like something and benefit from it. You aren't slamming down your fist on a table making demands or shouting empty promises. You're simply making *suggestions*. Suggestions by their very nature are non-threatening. The expectation you've "planted" in their minds is that of a comforting experience. That is where hypnosis enters in. You're predicting that the listener will be very pleased and happy. As soon as you tell the person that, you subtly trigger their imagination. They will conjure up their images like a warm beach, a gentle breeze, a pleasant smell, a delicious meal, a calming musical note.

| | |
|---|---|
| valuable<br>dream<br>pleasurable<br>e-e-e-easy<br>how happy you will feel<br>wouldn't it be great if…<br>enjoyable<br>comfortable | The words to the left are triggers of positive emotions you can employ when promoting your service, delivering your message or selling your product. The listener is coaxed into imagining a pleasurable experience they've had in the past. It is like evoking a fond memory. |

No one can reject the desirability of experiencing what the words on the left represent. Everyone wants something valuable. Everyone has a dream. Everyone wants a pleasurable experience. Everyone likes things to be easy. Everyone likes to imagine. Everyone wants to be soothed at times. Everyone wants life to been enjoyable. Everyone wants to be happy. Everyone wants to be comfortable. Throughout the whole presentation, you're going to use repetition, the father of learning.

Hypnotists "walk" the listener through the process. In this case, it is a buying process. It could also be a process by which people are influenced to follow you. Ronald Reagan, Martin Luther King, and – unfortunately – Hitler did it effectively. They did so by inducing their listeners to feel pleased with themselves, and feel special.

This chapter does not recommend that sellers of a product or idea put their buyers into an eerie trance or fool people into doing what they wouldn't normally want to do. However, a seller can influence their listeners through the power of persuasion. Although the pedestrian rationale for doing so would be the profit motive, it isn't that at all. Persuasion leads people to do what is suggested because they feel it will be of benefit to themselves. The outcome is a win-win situation because both the seller and the buyer are happy.

Milton H. Erickson was a psychiatrist, a psychologist, a family therapist, and a hypnotist. He created a foundation, the American Society for Clinical Hypnosis. Erickson also held a series of notable roles including fellowships in the American Psychiatric Association, The American Psychological Association, and the American Psychopathological Association. His pivotal principle was the power of the unconscious mind to alter behavior.

## Using Mind Control for Persuasion

### Social Pressure to Influence Behavior

Let's say that a group of students is given a test. No set time is presented in which to finish. After a short time, two students finish the test and turn it in. What happens? The rest of the students speed up, and then more stand up. The more frequently that happens, the faster the papers are turned in. Even the student who is still struggling with the test will usually stand up and pass in the test, even though he didn't answer all the questions and he didn't run out of time. Why is that? He didn't want to appear "different," or "stupid" or "odd." It's what is called the "herd mentality."

You see that in what are called trends. Let's say people start bringing home small dogs. More and more small dogs suddenly show up on the sidewalks at dog-walking time. They're "popular," you conclude. Are they really? Or are people adopting small dogs because it's the trend? Think about it. Suppose someone shows up with a Saint Bernard at dog-walking time. What happens? Everyone stares at him. Then they look more closely. They notice perhaps that he's wearing light-colored pants. They notice he has a long-sleeve sweater on. Then you conclude that he's odd, and his clothes are odd. They're not, of course, but you've been programmed to jump to the conclusion that everything about the man is odd.

You don't want to be associated with him. You want to be "one of the crowd." It helps you feel comfortable and accepted. The human desire to belong is a very powerful one. So is the power of social persuasion.

Everyone conforms to the unwritten code of social behavior and expression.

## Psychological Pressure Influences Behavior

Let's say there's an office party held at regular intervals. New employees are encouraged to come, and the person who invites them talks about how much fun it is and what a rip-roaring good time everyone had at the last party. What happens? The new employees go – but what if the party is boring? Nevertheless, they come and come again. Why? Because they don't want to be left out. They persist in coming because they have been influenced to believe that they will have a great time soon. Now, what has happened? It wasn't only the power of social persuasion that influenced the employees; it was the power of psychological persuasion.

Mob mentality is built upon social and psychological persuasion. A young man takes a can of paint and sprays hateful words on the walls of a city building. Then, another graffiti insult appears. In time, the whole building is lined up with people covering the walls full of insulting and even obscene comments. Each graffiti artist tries to outdo the other.

Yet, if you were to ask one of those people, just one of them, to put some graffiti on a clean wall, what would happen? Most likely he wouldn't do it. Why? Because he was alone. Earlier he had no problem doing it because was able to hide under the cloak of anonymity.

## Personal Pressure in Product Sales

Have you ever seen a table set up in a store with someone in a bright cap and an apron demonstrating a simple product like a cloth that absorbs liquid better than a sponge? He's lively, excited, and personable. A crowd gathers around to watch the performance. What happens at the end? Many customers buy the product. The demonstrator has used social persuasion to sell the product. It works well. However, when the product is simply left there sitting sedately on the shelf, few are attracted to it.

Using peer pressure in sales: A one-man job —

---

### Guy

Guy worked for many years in the back of an appliance store. He sold products like washing machines, dryers, dishwashers, and vacuum cleaners. Customers asked for him upon entering the store! How did he achieve that reputation?

Guy would first size up a couple who approached him, determine age and even their approximate income by their manner of dress. He used all the techniques elucidated at the beginning of this book. First, he'd smile broadly. He'd quickly <u>learn their names</u>; then carry on light conversations. He'd leave plenty of time for the customers to do the talking as they indicated what they wanted. He used all the methods of <u>active listening</u> by clarifying and asking questions about the customers' needs.

Let's say they wanted a vacuum cleaner. In his assessment, he noted that the woman was older, so he selected a model that was light and easy to handle.

"This is one of my most *popular* models, *Mary,*" he would say. "I just sold one to a lovely woman in Millersville. She was delighted with it. In fact, I have one like this at home!"

There, Guy introduced three powerful concepts – that of recalling the customer's name, social pressure, (the word "popular,") and psychological pressure ("I have one like that at home").

How does the psychological pressure enter in?

It is a truism that potential customers want to buy, especially from a "nice and friendly" salesman like Guy, and especially from someone with direct experience with the product.

> (The truth of the matter is that Guy may not have that vacuum cleaner in his home, but he was convincing, wasn't he? That happens in nearly every automotive salesroom. It's interesting to note that – somehow – the salesperson you approach just so happens to own the same model and make you're interested in buying!)

Those same earlier customers returned again and again to the appliance store. They specifically asked for Guy. Guy sold them not only a vacuum cleaner but a washing machine, a dryer, an air conditioner, and a dishwasher!

Another tool cited by Dale Carnegie was the power of testimony. When a customer hears that others like him or she liked the product or the proposal, they, too, want it. That is an application of social or peer pressure in sales. Note TV commercials. Many, many of them use that technique.

Know your target audience. Are they young people? The elderly? Middle-class, lower-class or the wealthy? Tailor your approach accordingly.

Unlike what commercials say, the product doesn't "sell itself." You sell *yourself!*

**The Nudge Theory**

In the year 2008, Cass Sunstein and Richard Thaler of the University of Chicago developed a method of sprinkling one's external and mental environment with very subtle suggestions that were influential in altering individual behavior. It works on one's cognition and senses, and causes people to make preordained decisions. It isn't mesmerism as in traditional hypnosis, but it strongly influences a person's behavior, much like a forced-choice examination does when students are "forced" to choose between options A, B, C, or D. According to its creators, "A nudge, as we will use the term, is any aspect of the choice architecture that alters people's behavior in a predictable way without forbidding any options or significantly changing their economic incentives. To count as a mere nudge, the intervention must be easy and cheap to avoid. Nudges are not mandates. Putting fruit at eye level counts as a nudge. Banning junk food does not." It is similar to social pressure, but can also be applied to individuals depending upon the context.

A mundane example of a nudge would be the placement of candy or magazines next to the cash register. Watch people at the grocery store. They politely line up in single file at the registers. Ads always use the word "save." The use of that word is actually illogical. If you *spend* money on an item, you're not *saving* it! However, people have been conditioned to understand that it means the price that's listed is less than the average price for that item elsewhere. The word acts according to the Stimulus-Response principle first elucidated by B.F. Skinner. You see the word, and you respond by making the choice of buying it. "Nudges" are intended to coax you to make a choice.

Nudges utilize sensory input. They operate like signals. Listen to a few TV commercials. Note how many contain the ringing of doorbells. That's intended to gain your immediate attention as doorbells do.

Associate visual imagery with choice. With a wink of orange waving against a serene violet backdrop, the banner undulated in the gentle breeze. Regardless of what the banner signifies, you like the banner, don't you? Work on words that conjure up a mood, and you'll influence your audience. Carefully choose your words. Suppose you said the banner "*flapped* in the gentle breeze." The mood is destroyed.

**Promoting Desirable Behaviors**

"Nudging" is less intrusive than mandating ideal societal behaviors. The social environment is the prime mover of choice rather than the rational mind. The British government created a unit called the Behavioral Insights Team whose function it is to create "prompts" or "nudges" to encourage better choice-making on the part of its citizens. It is a more pleasant alternative than passing a law.

It was proven to be successful with the HMRC (Her Majesty's Revenue and Customs), the British version of America's IRS. In their late notices, the HMRC sent out a carefully worded letter implying that the majority of those people living in the recipient's neighborhood paid on time.

A similar phenomenon happened in the United States. People were encouraged to recycle. Municipalities then gave out free containers and were also given days on which they could put them out at the end of their driveways. That alone wouldn't encourage people to recycle. HOWEVER, when people noticed that their neighbors were doing it, it operated as an incentive. When they were informed that the township wouldn't raise their taxes if a larger proportion of the population recycled, even more recyclables were carted down to the end of driveways.

**Choice and Behavioral Economics**

Human behavior is ideally determined by a rational choice. When options are presented, it would be expected that people will choose what's best for them, that is, the decision that maximizes their sense of satisfaction. Behavioral economics explores why people may choose what is NOT in their best interest. Why would they make irrational decisions? Because of the tremendous power of peer influence and the all-too-human tendency toward conformity. It is the opposite of individual choice and depends upon the herd mentality.

<u>The Lizard Brain</u>

In the 1960s, Paul McLean first introduced the term "lizard brain." It refers to the brain stem of the human being which controls the basic survival instinct – the fight-flight response triggered by a surge of the hormone, adrenaline. It allows people to react quickly and efficiently when in the process of decision-making. The term has been applied to behavioral economics, and is a powerful predictor of how people will respond to advertising, promotion, and marketing. Leaders, the "shakers and the movers," the trendsetters of society pivot their approach upon this. It is like the universal joint in an automobile upon which the wheel is based. There's no movement without it.

A similar thing happens in investment. If a day trader hears that a particular stock is going to sky-rocket, he or she will be influenced to make the rash decision of buying it. People have the tendency to believe that they will definitely succeed. Huge lotteries attract more people when they are heavily advertised. Common sense, though, dictates that one's chances of winning are significantly reduced when more and more people buy tickets.

Predominance in the Dual-System of the Brain

Aristotle explained that people utilize two systems of thought. System 1 refers to the engagement of one's "lizard brain," and System 2 is the logical brain. In System 2, human beings arrive at a decision through a deductive process of reasoning. In terms of advertising, System 1 prevails and leads to System 2 by which choices are subjected to a reasoning procedure. For example, someone will choose between a two-wheel or a four-wheel drive depending on need and use.

## The Brain Bias

People prefer to think of themselves as unbiased. That isn't true. Instantaneously, people make decisions based on a myriad of audiovisual inputs. For example, a person can make a decision as to whether or not someone is a threat based upon facial expressions, dress, bodily position, and even speed of walking. Critics have indicated that this is an unrealistic concept, as it implies people develop preferences ahead of time.

For example, if a woman on a diet is informed about the caloric count of particular foods, her rational choice should be to choose only low calorie foods. However, if she is presented with pictures of delicious ice cream, she may weaken and eat a large dish of ice cream. That's because of the bias aspects of decision-making.

In economic terms, even if the dieting woman is told that the ice cream is on sale at an attractive price, and is even less expensive than a fruited dessert, she may be influenced by 1) her own preference for the ice cream, and 2) her obsession on weight.

## Harnessing the Biases

Desired behaviors can be elicited by recognizing that there will be biases, and that people will choose the "easy way out." For instance, advertisers and promoters will provide two options, but "rig" the choice by placing the preferred option as a default and the other choice as an "opt-out" feature. People then appreciate the fact they have a choice, but the majority of them will select the default.

An unusual artifact occurs when the majority of people "jump on the bandwagon" by making the most popular choice. This results in the disruption of the Law of Supply and Demand. The choice of consumers doesn't depend upon personal preference and/or price. The choice depends upon the choices others made. That has strong implications in political campaigns because people want to be on the "winning side" of an election.

<u>Empathy</u>

The more successful promoters mentally put themselves into the shoes of their subjects, and objectively analyze how they themselves would respond if presented with the appeal of the seller or promoter.

**Relativity Traps**

A recent example of this is the advertisement that a detergent contains "OXY" (oxygen). More people will opt to buy the detergent that has the word "OXY" on it. It "sounds" good. In reality, *all* soaps contain oxygen atoms in equal amounts. The word "save," discussed earlier, is another example of this. In truth, a person depends upon assumptions that haven't been corroborated. In the soap case, people weren't informed that all detergents contain oxygen and in the second example, people don't know the actual price of the product and have nothing with which to compare prices.

## Choice Overload

If a person is presented with a package offering a course, for example, and given a choice which is the course plus video presentations and a mailed piece - in other words, the full package - most people choose that option as opposed to the abridged package, which is less expensive. Why is that? A person would choose the former because of a factor called "decision overload." They don't want to spend the time analyzing the package and fear the loss of certain features. In a study performed by Eric Bettinger in conjunction with H&R Block, a streamlined version of the student aid form increased college enrollment 8%, as opposed to aid forms that were lengthy.

## Loss Aversion

We are "loss averse." We tend to put more effort into avoiding losses than to receive gains from a purchase. When President Obama introduced the Affordable Care Act, he presented the American people with two choices: 1) purchase health insurance or 2) incur a penalty for not doing so. His strategy took advantage of influencing decisions because people are loss averse. They purchased the insurance rather than incur the penalty. In actuality, the penalty was less than the insurance, but people rejected that and bought the insurance. (In 2017, the Republicans repealed it in a new tax bill.)

In the stock market, people more frequently choose a low-return stock portfolio because it is more likely to guarantee returns, even though they are modest ones. People tend to shy away from risky investments, even though they might yield higher gains. In that case, they are "risk averse."

## The Impact of Nudges

When trying to influence decision-making, governments often use the principles of the Nudge Theory. The traditional approaches of rebates and the like offered to persuade people to modify their behaviors and choices were far less effective than providing people with measurements of the behavior of peers. For example, a township tried to influence people to conserve by mailing them flyers that showed how their use of gas compared to that of their neighbors. Although the residents didn't receive a rebate for reduced use, there was a far greater response to reduce usage as compared to the traditional rebate method.

## Peer Pressure: Online Selling

Peer pressure can work well in online selling. After you've developed the graphic aspects (Logo, short introduction), add comments from real or imagined prior customers. Too much attention is often paid to logos. They will never communicate higher-level concepts. Simplicity is the key. Use a persuasive introductory photo….two people shaking hands, for example. Many companies use photos of their friendly workers. Fewer is better than an army of workers. (That looks expensive. No customer wants to pay all their salaries!)

Feedback is essential. When you start selling, ask your friends and relatives to post five-star reviews for you, or hire some people to do it for you. Quote the most notable ones. For instance: "I was delighted with _____. My friends and neighbors complimented me and bought it for themselves. - Suzie G. from Cincinnati." Put a number of them in. "I thought that the team did a fine job on my lawn. It looked manicured. They cleaned up after themselves too, and it took only a short time for them to complete the job." Put those quotes right up front. Many don't do that, but it is the most effective way to attract immediate interest.

Simplicity is usually the best approach for feedback remarks because the feedback sounds genuine. Have your website designer avoid the use of tables. Not all search engines parse the data in such a way that the content ***with the keywords*** can be read. Have them avoid templates. Repeat the keywords and use a number of similar words: "comfortable," "soft," "plush." Put your personal touch into the presentation. Use your photo or you and your partners' photos. If you don't feel as if you're good-looking enough, how about your nephews/nieces or your cousins? Swear them to silence!

In text, sometimes there needs to be a break in the all-too-familiar one-word-after-the other paragraph-after-paragraph. Break up the text with boxes, colors, photos, cartoons, and different size fonts. It may cost more, but it's well worth the expense.

Review the use of keywords earlier in this book and place them in apropos places. Check out your competition and try to locate the most repeated words about your product or service. The search engines will seek them out when placing the position of your ad. It also should be mentioned here that some search engines have services to place your ad above others – for a fee, of course. Some also sell keywords. Compare the approaches of your competition and put yourself in the customers' shoes. Which ones are the most appealing and why?

Apply the same techniques that you read about earlier in this chapter – peer pressure (it's popular) and psychological pressure, this time, featuring the rewards the customer will experience in buying from you (incentives).

> Above all, keep this in mind – The quality of your product is essential, HOWEVER, it is *seldom the quality* of what you are selling that will result in good sales. It is *your persuasive power and marketing strategy* that will lead to success.

Develop two or possibly three different sales presentations on the Internet. You can put them up simultaneously, as with selling a series of books, or periodically introduce new presentations with the same sales pitches. That depends, of course, on the nature of your product or service.

You might also want to purchase a deal where you can run small ads that run to the right side of websites. You will have to pay a fee "per hit" for most of them.

Selling on the internet requires marketing and capital. If you are going to use a marketing firm, select one that's been in business a *long* time. Renew your contract with them. Again, this will be expensive.

# Chapter 8- Persuasion and Influence

## In-Person Persuasion: The Framework
- **Preparing for the Launch**

When you are engaged in making an in-person verbal presentation, followed by a proposal, **warm-up exercises** will help you get your "juices flowing." The best-known sales coach of all time – Dale Carnegie – did them, and recommended them for his students. Public speakers do them routinely. Look up some *easy exercises* on the Internet and – as silly as you might feel – do them! Use your voice either in talking, shouting, or singing.

***Chew*** on something before you make a verbal presentation. Chewing and eating is an enjoyable experience. In nursing homes and hospitals, dinner time is the quietest time on the floor. Even people in discomfort or pain tend to be quiet. Chewing reduces the anxiety people associate with disease.

***Dance exercises*** are usually the least personally threatening. Find a comfortable video and follow along as best you can. Do it in front of a mirror, and practice smiling and singing. They don't have to be intense cardio workouts; just something simple, but move around the room. This puts your mind into an outgoing mode of communication. You can even practice doing your sales pitch to some lively musical score.

- **The Stage**

    The stage for making a personal presentation differs. It could be that you're preparing a TED talk and your stage is the Internet. Your stage could be a gathering, like a party. Your stage could be more modest like chatting with a few friends over your cell phone. It could be digital, as on a website or in a blog. It could be a Kindle book.

- **The Idea**

    Your mind is chock full of ideas. To persuade people, you need to deliver a *single* idea. Therefore, take a journey around your mind, and single out an idea about which you are most passionate. Narrow down the setting in which your idea operates. It could have as its theme personal growth, technology, motivation, inspiration, nature or entertainment. In your initial presentation, formulate your sentences so that they focus back on that theme. All your words are connected by that single idea.

- **Reason to Care**

    Your aim is to persuade people to think about the idea/theme the same way you think about it. So, you need to give your listeners a reason to care about it. Present examples. Pulling upon people's heartstrings when talking about critical social issues is a strong motivating factor. After all, you want people to want to join you in doing it.

Humans are, by nature, curious. Ring that bell within their minds. Ask rhetorical questions. Let's say you want to persuade people to design an app that will do an activity without leading them through a 'gazillion' steps to complete the activity.

- **Use Familiar Concepts and Metaphors**

Use concepts with which everyone is familiar. Many new trends invent terms to explain their ideas. This isn't always the best approach unless you are trying to sell the concept. For example, the question "Do you use a 'pulse pack'?" The speaker here uses a term with which people are not familiar. The speaker is selling a term, not an idea *unless* he or she uses metaphors or familiar visual concepts to elucidate the usage. For example, you might explain that the 'pulse pack' is *like* fingers massaging your neck…muscles….legs. The speaker has used the metaphor *"like"* using a familiar image (fingers) to explain their massage device.

- **Purpose**

Your idea has to be worth sharing. It can be a sentiment and an idea that has a useful purpose. For example, an app that separates your email into categories automatically. Everyone who gets useful information that the user has to reorganize would love to have a device that automatically puts it into your related folders.

What about something more esoteric? It might be a

value that's sorely needed, for example, the need to reduce bullying in the workplace, help someone feel better about themselves, convince someone that they can do what they've always wanted to do...or get mighty close to achieving that goal. Believe this and it will be so!

- **The Great Cause**

Look deep down in your heart, and explore your marvelous mind. Care...really care about your audience. Create the mindscape you know they want to have by subscribing to your service or manipulating your product. You're there to make them leave your presence happier than they were before. Eradicate the feeling that you are being pressured by your goals. You are you and it is you who can mold the minds of your listeners as if they were made of clay.

Think of what makes people want to perform these actions the way *YOU* want them to, as opposed to the way other people or companies do it. You CAN do that...you really can.

Your approach is INNOVATIVE...It is DIFFERENT from the status quo. Moreover, it is a CAUSE worth fighting for.

You are not simply selling an approach, a message or a product – how pedestrian that is! You're selling WHY you're doing it. You're selling the fact that you are ***different***, you are ***innovative***, and you have a ***cause.***

You're selling the *value* of your message.

Not only that, but you are triggering loyalty. A person will prefer to buy your product, adopt your techniques, as opposed to those of others, because you have evoked their loyalty. They also *liked* you, as they liked Guy in Chapter 7.

According to Stephen Sinek, the leadership coach, "People don't buy what you do; they buy *why* you do it." To that add this codicil: They are buying what *you* represent.

People who believe what you as the leader believe, will do as you do. They want to be a part of that movement and will join in by buying your product or service.

Martin Luther King didn't produce a plan; he produced a belief. It was he who said "I have a dream," not "I have a plan."

**Link**

There is an intimate link between imagination and reality. Use vivid imagery to describe your project or product. Speak slowly and deliberately. Once the visual picture is inside the listener's mind, he or she claims it as their own. They begin to think it's their own idea, although it is yours. It's now internalized.

People begin to personalize the image. They carefully "paint" the picture in their mind's eye, and apply it to choices they make in the future.

**Different**

The public opinion dictates that you have to think like everyone else. While there is some truth to the rewards of conformity, it's OK to be different than others, especially in your thinking. Do different things. For example, most women don't wear hats. Wear a hat, then. It could become your trademark.

---

<u>True Story:</u>     Larry's Bike

Larry had a difficult time learning how to balance himself on a bicycle. He became extremely upset about it and developed feelings of inferiority because of it. He isolated himself and didn't play with the other children in the neighborhood.

His father came up with an ingenious solution. He built the boy a four-wheeled red bike. It took the father a long time to coax his son to ride it, but eventually he started to. No sooner did Larry show up with his bike, then every child in the neighborhood wanted to try out the bike. Larry wouldn't let them initially, but then they ran alongside him and begged him to let them try it out.

Eventually, Larry did, but was selective in letting certain children try out the bike. The side effect of this was the fact that Larry began to feel he was popular, and – in reality – he *did* become popular. He learned that it's OK to be different. Little by little he came out of himself, and joined the others in baseball and football games. He also never lost the reward of being different and unusual.

---

**State of Mind**

All performers are accustomed to assessing the state of mind of their audience. It is a honed skill to determine the moods of the people you're addressing. Some performers use a light-hearted joke to kick off, especially when an audience is glaring at them critically. Create a mental box of memorized light-hearted remarks. Some performers make comments about the town or location of their performance. Familiarize yourself ahead of time. Be sure there's sufficient lighting without blasting your audience out of the room.

**Give and Take**

A casual study at a restaurant revealed that there was a correlation between the giving of dinner mints and the size of the tips. Some interesting results occurred. When one mint was given at the end of the meal, the tip increased by 3%. When two mints were given, tips didn't double; they quadrupled to 14%. However, when the waitress gave one mint and walked away; then paused, returned, and said, "For you nice people, here's an extra mint," tips increased by 23%!

There is an old adage: "You can attract more flies with honey than with vinegar." People can and do respond to gentle persuasion, especially when accompanied by kindness. The moral of this tale is the fact that the giving was personable and unexpected.

Show caring and kindness in your presentation. If you have something like a preliminary booklet, hand it out at the beginning of your presentation. Many websites do that. Be sure that what you give is valuable enough to attract interest, not a mere token.

**Solicit Questions from your Subjects**

Present the general topic of your presentation or proposal. Engage your listeners right away by asking them what they expect from the session. Actively listen as is explained in Chapter 4. Memorize the words that were most frequently used, and regurgitate them throughout your presentation. You may be quite surprised and enlightened by the issues your audience brings up. This technique will also give you an idea about the intellectual level of your audience. Ask a few people in the audience about their occupations. That way, you can tailor your approach to the discussion of the benefits your product or service will deliver.

Not only should you solicit questions, but put on a "happy face" and a welcoming expression when you do so. Remember, there are cognitive aspects involved here. You are appealing to a person's thought process.

Mentally, the sharing of information and asking of questions helps people feel knowledgeable and important. Social cognition entails working the medial Prefrontal Cortex (mPFC) of the brain. It has neural connections that lead to the emotional centers of the brain, indicating that people are associating the answers to the questions in an emotional context. This is ideal, as you know that your subjects are truly listening and making judgments, including value judgments. In other words, you are reaching them. They are also considering themselves using your process or product in their social environment.

> *A Little Hint—*
>
> When you're looking at a questioner or a member of your audience, look just slightly above at the bridge between the eyebrows. From the other person's perspective, you appear to be looking straight at them. They then know they have your full attention. Be cautious, though. If it's a long-winded question, glance to the side just once in a while. Maintaining an eye-to-eye look too long can be disconcerting.
>
> That area of the head is called the "third eye," by many Eastern philosophers. They believe it is the window to the soul. Of course, you're not teaching parapsychology or religion, but the old wisdom has some application here. You are "touching" the subconscious minds of your listeners in a very real way. According to Taoist thinking, the Third Eye is the main energy center of the body and is located directly between the left and right hemispheres of the brain. The left brain controls logic and objective cognition and the right brain is the emotional center. Your presentation is directed toward both of those areas of the brain. Cognitively, you're presenting facts, but you also want to stimulate the positive emotions of your listeners. So, do not discount this practice. After all, you truly want to touch the mind of your listeners in both a cognitive and emotional way.

There is a well-known actor (name withheld) who had the habit of looking at one eye and then the other. His habit became so pronounced that his pupils were like ping-pong balls. It was immensely distracting. In time, he has conquered the habit, as – no doubt – his director noted it. It is tempting to get sucked into that habit yourself, so be careful.

Listen to many speakers' introductions. "Steal" a few jokes, after making some slight changes to avoid copyright issues. Watch live performances. Good speakers/comedians are very skilled in handling unexpected events. On one occasion, a salesman was making a presentation in New Jersey, but an annoying fly kept circling his head. This fly was, no doubt, one of the most stubborn insects in the Northeast! After he flicked his arm several times, the salesman stopped, looked straight out at the audience, and said, "That, ladies and gentlemen, is my very first customer! He's coming back for another package!"

## Scarcity

The luxury high-speed aircraft, the Concorde, ceased operations in 2003. It flew at a speed of 1,354 mph, twice the speed of sound. Naturally, that cut the flying time in half. The drawback was the fact that one transatlantic flight cost $12,000 round-trip. The extremely wealthy could afford it, but it certainly wasn't economical, even for those people. Also, there was a horrible fatal crash in 2000, killing all 109 passengers.

As the Concorde airplane aged, the maintenance costs skyrocketed. Based on that and the other factors mentioned, Air France and British Airways announced the Concorde flights would be permanently suspended.

Something strange happened after the announcement. The day after that, bookings on the Concorde skyrocketed! Why? When people see that a desired product or service is scarce, they go into a buying panic. Similar events happen when stores discontinue a particular product or right before a snowstorm.

The lesson here is clear: Tell your customers not only about the benefits and uniqueness of your product or service, but the deleterious effects they would undergo if they were to lose those benefits.

---

### Exercise

Use your active listening skills and turn on your TV. Listen to the commercials. Write down all the words that imply a shortage.

Some common examples are:

"Supplies are limited…"

"Offer expires…"

"Free for the first order…"

---

Another favorite word employed by advertisers is "**NOW**." It implies that a shortage may occur.

The word, usually expressed verbally or on a recording, is said in such a way that implies an upcoming change, like discontinuation or expiration of the benefits the product offers. It implies impending scarcity.

**Authority**

People can also be persuaded when the seller has or seems to have a level of authority. That is, if they are perceived as experts. Imagine what would happen if you went into a gym, and the trainers and even the receptionists were sloppy. The place would close the day it opened! When you are presenting a proposal, dress in clothing suitable for your service. A business proposal is usually presented by someone in a business suit.

The speaker also found some way to manifest his credentials. There are two other alternatives to that – having someone else introduce you, and they cite your experience and credentials. The speaker can also quote from studies related to their proposal, or more commonly, facets of their presentation that imply that you, as the speaker, are moving in a positive direction.

By implementing supportive material and others who will testify on your behalf, you can increase interest and sales by 20%.

There is more to presenting a proposal than a cosmetic appearance. The speaker needs to be excellent at public speaking. He or she might bring in charts or a writing board. The background used for presentations makes a tremendous difference. That depends upon the theme of your presentation, although you might have to risk elimination of some of its features for practical reasons. Avoid bright white. It's reminiscent of a doctor's office.

Some brave presenters present their work without embellishments. In that case, you and you alone are the center of interest. Provide "embellishments" like fluid movements and gestures. Above all, SOUND EXCITED about your project.

The noted motivational speaker, Tony Robbins, always uses a background that relates to the theme of his presentation. In one of his YouTube presentations, it showed Robbins in a boat on a serene lake. He was addressing the issue of helping yourself feel peaceful and happy. The video communicated success, as well as peace. He used the word "success" repeatedly. He also smiled throughout the video. The gentle background sent the message of peace and Robbins' smile communicated "happy."

**Like You – Like Me**

People can be more easily persuaded when they can personally identify with the speaker. This is called "implicit egotism." It is an unconscious desire to talk to people or have things and experiences that associate with themselves.

Many salespeople use chit-chat for that. It's an effort to find some commonalities between the speaker and the audience. In the Tony Robbins' video discussed above, Tony wasn't on a yacht; he appeared to be in a simple rowboat and was dressed casually. Most people have been in rowboats and dress casually.

People are more likely to be influenced by people like themselves, especially those whom they admire. The statistics of studies conducted on surveys related to the effectiveness of testimonials differ widely, usually ranging anywhere from 70 to 92%. Many people who had read reviews of products and services on websites said they were influenced by a majority of positive responses in terms of trust level.

Testimonials are like word-of-mouth verbal testimonials. No one wants to be the guinea pig. In terms of verbal proposals, it's important to ask people that they spread the word. If they say something particularly complimentary, ask if you may quote them, assuring them that they'll remain anonymous, or relatively so, like saying something to the effect of "Betty from the Bronx said she not only used my product, but her neighbors bought it too."

## Testimonials

Studies have shown that the testimonial has around a 70% impact upon purchasing. People dislike being guinea pigs. Quoted testimonials are extremely effective. When a peer recommends something, this awakens the tendency that most people have toward implicit egotism. It also explains why teenagers have similar types of dress. They want to be associated with those products and services that their peers use. Social testimonials are those done unexpectedly. They haven't been requested nor asked for. For example, one comes into a restaurant because others recommended it. The restaurant owners never approached the general public requesting it.

On the Internet, this occurs on Facebook, Instagram, Twitter or another social media outlet. A video testimonial is very powerful. This occurs when someone outside of the company makes a YouTube video or the like about a product or service. When someone unknown does that, it can be very powerful because it's not likely to be faked. Interview videos are also used. In those, the interviewer is seen, but the interviewee is sometimes off-screen. In some cases, both are shown. When the latter occurs, people will carefully examine the visual cues on the part of the interviewee and assess whether or not the facial reactions of the interviewee appear genuine. Influencer testimonials are testimonials given by celebrities. These are hired endorsements. Companies seek out individuals who are generally trusted in the field.

**Valuation**

Valuation has to do with the promoter or seller. The first person to convince of the value of a product or proposal is yourself. You, as a promoter, need to examine your package or product carefully and be convinced that it's valuable to your audience. The more valuable you feel it is, the more likely you are to convince others of the value.

This calls for a salient, logical presentation, citing some of the features, benefits, and rewards of the product or process. The reward, though, isn't the money. It needs to be something that will enhance the well-being or "feel-good" aspects that will please people if they can achieve or own what you're promoting.

If there are drawbacks a person might experience while using your product or engaging in your process, be aware of them. Most sales are followed by questions and concerns about the use of the process or product. Be honest, and have simple solutions ready for these possible questions.

Once you're convinced of the value of your product or service, learn to convey the positive emotions you feel regarding the proposal or product to another. Because it makes you feel better about yourself share that with the other person. This you will show in your expressions – smile broadly – and manifest the calmness the process or product brought to you when you assessed its value. Sincerity is important, so if you're trying to promote something you are ambiguous about, try switching to something else.

You are happy to be sharing this process/product with others.

You are confident that it will have the same positive effect on them as it did on you.

It will resolve or fulfill whatever needs or wants the other will have.

People generally want to please others, because people are likely to respond positively toward you personally in return. Above all, look pleased that your audience had the courtesy to watch your presentation.

*Hint:* If your presentation is to be spoken, take a course in public speaking and practice in front of a mirror or with friends. Eliminate the clumsy "ah's and um's" in your speech. Use friendly gestures, but don't rock back and forth like a seesaw. Notice how no one on a TV show does that. It takes practice because the "um's" give the impression that you're not sure about the proposal or product. It also conveys the fact that you're nervous. That's difficult to overcome for people who tend to be shy. Never use the phrase, "You know what I mean…" or "like…you know."

## The Neural Activity of Successful Persuaders

Those who've developed good skills at selling an idea or a product show a high development of the temporoparietal junction. That is an area of the brain that acts as a traffic manager. Information enters the gifted speaker first through his or her senses (visual and auditory), and the person processes information from the external environment, like the body language and facial responses of his or her subjects; coordinates it and reaches a conclusion about the listening subjects. Activity in that area is crucial in what is called the "Theory of the Mind." That stimulates the person's sense of empathy and understanding of their audience.

Successful persuaders actually *care* about the people they are engaging with. It's certainly true that you want your listeners to feel the same sense of satisfaction you derive from using your process or product. The successful persuader isn't merely interested in the money they'll make from it. The money is just the side effect of the process of persuasion itself.

There is only a fine line of distinction between a vivid imaginative idea and the real idea. When describing the process that will occur if your listeners adopt your procedure, use uplifting terms. Compliment your audience and give them credit for being thinking, feeling, and intelligent people. Tell them that they have the power and presence you display and can learn how to demonstrate it.

Read the following excerpt, and note what thoughts and emotions it conveys:

> You, brave and honorable people, have chosen to break into the green expanse of the future. Knowing not what comes, you will proceed with the courage and stamina of one human being, and confront the reality of tomorrow. It is your pledge to achieve the farther reaches of your potential. You will do it, even if it is hard to do. Yes, you will taste the fear of the unknown but will walk with one foot in front of the other like determined soldiers on the march. And, with

> every step you take – you will discover the secret of those who walked before you – that through vulnerability comes strength.

Use powerful words in your proposal. "You" is a vital word and bears a lot of repeating. Use inspiring words, and give your listener the gift of recognizing that they can be powerful, courageous, and have stamina, too. Admit to your listener that their journey will be difficult, and it will be hard. Balance it by assuming your subjects will come through with flying colors. Use words of commitment like "pledge." Create a visualization like that of a soldier going into battle, simply by placing one foot in front of the other. Then wind up by telling them that the outcome of their journey will be the achievement of reaching their full potential.

When promoting a product, choose adjectives like those in the following list:

| | |
|---|---|
| Awesome | Marvelous |
| Astonishing | Mind-blowing |
| Audacious | Miraculous |
| Breathtaking | Phenomenal |
| Brilliant | Remarkable |
| Daring | Splendid |
| Delightful | Valiant |

| Empowering | Radiant |
|---|---|
| Fabulous | Classy |
| Incredible | Eye-opening |

Skills of Persuasion

***Be assertive.*** There is a fine line between being assertive and being aggressive. Use "I's" in your presentation. You have already gone through the process of learning how to value what you're promoting or selling, so use yourself as an example. When presenting a proposal about a technique to build self-confidence, for example, speakers/writers admit that they were once shy and nervous. Because you're now coming across as assertive, people will know that your process works. Of course, keep in mind that you need to come across as a person just like them, so dress the part.

***Tell Them How.*** Realize that your proposal may be different from that which your subjects are accustomed to, so be explanatory. For instance, you might say "I'll show you how you can do this with ease." **Never** use the phrase "you should." That's for children.

***Like your listeners.*** This can be a challenge if you happen to have the misfortune of confronting people with frowns, who have their arms folded as if they're closing themselves off, or look bored, or glance elsewhere in the room. Be friendly nonetheless. Compliment a few people for what you've noticed about them. Most people tend to downplay compliments. Disagree with them and reassert your compliment.

***Be consistent.*** Be sure that your body language and facial expressions match your words.

***Be prepared.*** Prepare yourself for what salesmen call customer objections. Look at it like this – they are thinking and evaluating. They are trying to picture themselves in the roles you've laid out for them. They feel there may be potential problems and will want those resolved. This is a healthy cognitive approach and it tells you that the customer is interested (or they wouldn't ask). If, for example, the person wonders about providing refills for your vacuum, you have the freedom to offer a set of them for free. Also, explain the advantages of having these refills, and provide the information they need to get them.

***Keep It Open-Ended.*** Give your subjects the option of returning for a "refresher course," or ask them to stay on later so you can handle more questions. People don't want the promotion or product to be a one-shot affair. In that vein, provide similar opportunities in the future to either hear other promotions on other themes, or other products along the same line. The point of this is NOT to have people come repeatedly! Instead, it will inform the person that they're not being *forced* to make a choice. What you're telling them is the fact that THEY HAVE THE CHOICE TO MAKE A CHOICE! You're giving them power and freedom. Everyone wants power and freedom. You just gave them something that's at the core of the human condition. You already told them they'll be happy with your product or service. It will lead them to ask themselves "Sure…why not?"

***Be Truthful.*** People despise being fooled, and many are suspicious that might be the case. Yes, you want to persuade others, but you want to be ethical about it.

***Pose Your Questions.*** You know your presentation and/or product. Therefore, you already have a good idea about what questions your audience might ask. Sometimes, they don't think of the more common ones, so it's helpful if you can foresee what those might be.

# Chapter 9 – Summing Up

We're ending here with Chapter 9, because you're going to act out Chapter 10. Forever believe because – as you believe – so you will be.

**The Problem with Reward**

Reread this book, as it can be lived over and over again as you change. Take the example of Tatiana. She was among a group of promoters, all of whom had their own tables. At the end of the day, the crowds had dissipated. However, Tatiana had a tremendous line of people at her table. They were buyers and many wanted even more products like the one she sold. As this occurred early in her career, she was astonished. However, it brought with it a responsibility. She had obviously sold something of great value. People wanted more. Success has a nagging side effect. It creates a motive where before there was only a modest one. Like a freight train leaving the station, your motive to continue will move faster and faster, giving rise to new and exciting ideas. You will get caught up in your own momentum.

So, too, will you remember that you must grow and change. You cannot permit your prior success to become a memory. It is an intimate part of you and now defines who you are.

www.ingramcontent.com/pod-product-compliance
Lightning Source LLC
Chambersburg PA
CBHW071453070526
44578CB00001B/328